The Glacier National Park, A Popular Guide to Its Geology and Scenery: USGS Bulletin 600

Marius R. Campbell

The BiblioGov Project is an effort to expand awareness of the public documents and records of the U.S. Government via print publications. In broadening the public understanding of government and its work, an enlightened democracy can grow and prosper. Ranging from historic Congressional Bills to the most recent Budget of the United States Government, the BiblioGov Project spans a wealth of government information. These works are now made available through an environmentally friendly, print-on-demand basis, using only what is necessary to meet the required demands of an interested public. We invite you to learn of the records of the U.S. Government, heightening the knowledge and debate that can lead from such publications.

Included are the following Collections:

Budget of The United States Government
Presidential Documents
United States Code
Education Reports from ERIC
GAO Reports
History of Bills
House Rules and Manual
Public and Private Laws

Code of Federal Regulations
Congressional Documents
Economic Indicators
Federal Register
Government Manuals
House Journal
Privacy act Issuances
Statutes at Large

DEPARTMENT OF THE INTERIOR

UNITED STATES GEOLOGICAL SURVEY

GEORGE OTIS SMITH, Director

BULLETIN 600

THE
GLACIER NATIONAL PARK

A POPULAR GUIDE TO ITS GEOLOGY AND SCENERY

BY

MARIUS R. CAMPBELL

WASHINGTON

GOVERNMENT PRINTING OFFICE

1914

CONTENTS.

ILLUSTRATIONS.

4

THE GLACIER NATIONAL PARK:
A POPULAR GUIDE TO ITS GEOLOGY AND SCENERY.

By Marius R. Campbell.

INTRODUCTION.

The Glacier National Park includes that part of the Front Range of the Rocky Mountains lying just south of the Canadian line, in Teton and Flathead counties, Mont. It is bounded on the west by Flathead River (locally called North Fork), on the south by the Middle Fork of Flathead River and the Great Northern Railway, and on the east by the Blackfeet Indian Reservation.

Although this part of the Rocky Mountains has been known since Lewis and Clark crossed the continent in 1805–6, the region later made a park appears not to have been visited by white men until 1853, when Cut Bank Pass was crossed by A. W. Tinkham, one of the Government engineers engaged in exploring a route for the Pacific railroad. Tinkham, who was encamped in the Bitterroot Valley, was ordered to examine Marias Pass, but in traversing Middle Fork of Flathead River along the line of the present railroad he was evidently misled by the large size of the valley of Nyack Creek and ascended that instead of keeping to the right up the main stream. He reported the pass impracticable for railroad construction, and so this region dropped out of public attention for a long time.

The next explorers to enter the region were a group of surveyors who, under the direction of American and British commissioners, established the international boundary line along the forty-ninth parallel from the Pacific coast to the main summit of the Rocky Mountains. This party reached the area now included in the park in the summer of 1861, and the stone monument shown in Plate I, *B*, which they erected on the Continental Divide west of Waterton Lake, still marks a point on the boundary between the United States and Canada.

The land on the west side of the range formed a part of the public domain which, until the erection of the park, was open to settlement, but the land on the east originally belonged to the Blackfeet Indians and the white men had no rights upon it. About 1890 copper ore was found near the heads of Quartz and Mineral creeks, and a great

5

boom for this region followed. Many prospectors drifted in, expecting to reap rich rewards from the discovery of mineral deposits and the general development of the region. Several of the main trails were built about this time, and considerable money was spent in prospecting, in opening mines, and in providing machinery to handle the large output of copper ore that was expected.

The copper-bearing veins were found to extend through the range to the east side, but prospecting in that part of the mountains was not possible, for the land was included in the Indian reservation. This situation produced a growing discontent among the prospectors, who began to have a strong feeling that the Government should come to their relief by acquiring the coveted land and placing it at their disposal. The urgent demand of the prospectors and promoters was felt in Congress, and a bill was passed providing for the purchase from the Indians of this supposed mineral land for $1,500,000. In accordance with this act, a treaty with the Blackfeet Indians was signed at Browning, Mont., September 26, 1895, and approved by the Senate on June 10, 1896, by which the west line of the reservation was removed from the Continental Divide and was fixed along the eastern points of the spurs of the mountain range, as shown on the accompanying map, and the land so acquired was thrown open to mineral entry only.

Under the stimulus of the new territory acquired, active prospecting was carried on for a time, but copper ore was found only in small quantities, and gradually the prospectors and miners drifted away to newer or more promising fields, and the region reverted to its original condition. For a long time it was visited only by hunters in search of big game and by summer visitors who, in order to escape the heat of the plains, were willing to undergo the privations and discomforts of the rude hotels then to be found in the region.

Although these mountains had ceased to interest prospectors in search of mineral wealth, they still possessed a fascination for the lovers of natural scenery and almost everyone who visited the region was impressed with its alpine beauty. Again it was brought to the attention of Congress, which was urged to secure it for the use of the people by setting it aside as a national park. On May 11, 1910, President Taft signed the bill creating the Glacier National Park, and this most interesting and beautiful region thus became a permanent playground for the American people.

GENERAL PHYSICAL FEATURES OF THE PARK.

The scenic features of the park are truly alpine in their character, consisting of a wonderful combination of rugged mountain tops bounded by vertical walls from a few hundred to more than 4,000 feet in height, many interesting glaciers perched along the range in

A. THOMAS JEFFERSON, ONE OF THE EARLY PROSPECTORS AND HUNTERS.

Mr. Jefferson came to this part of the country about 1882. Photograph by M. R. Campbell.

B. MONUMENT MARKING THE POINT WHERE THE INTERNATIONAL BOUNDARY CROSSES THE
CONTINENTAL DIVIDE, WEST OF WATERTON LAKE.

Looking southeast across the line into the United States. Monument set in 1861. Photograph by Bailey Willis.

protected places, beautifully timbered slopes leading down by graceful curves to the bottoms of the valleys, and scores of lakes that are unsurpassed by any to be found in sunny Italy or the more rugged regions of Switzerland. This rare combination of scenic beauty is found not alone in one valley of the park but is characteristic of them all, and it is difficult to single out any particular part that is more beautiful than another.

One of the most interesting things about the park is the fact that the peculiarly rugged topography described above is practically limited to the region included within its boundaries. If one travels to the point where the Canadian line crosses the Continental Divide he will see that north of the line the mountains gradually lose their scenic interest, consisting only of low rounded ridges that are destitute of the rugged features to be found in the park. If he journeys in the opposite direction he will find that south of the Great Northern Railway there is little of interest to be seen and that the mountains are only such as are common to the ranges he has crossed in making the transcontinental trip. Even to the traveler on the railway the park is a sealed book, for in an ordinary journey he sees nothing of its beauty except here and there a snow-covered peak that glistens in the sparkling air of the early morning or catches the dull red rays of the setting sun. He gets no idea of the beautiful lakes, the glaciers, nor the mountains themselves, and doubtless he wonders why this region should be called a playground for the people. But let him stop at Belton or at Glacier Park station and let him really see something of the beauties of Lake McDonald, Lake St. Mary, Bowman Lake, and then he can understand the attractive force that draws people across the continent and holds them spellbound before these awe-inspiring examples of nature's handiwork.

The dominant feature of the park is a broad mountain range trending in a northwesterly direction, on both sides of which there are areas of low relief. On the west the ascent to the top of the mountains is gradual, the traveler passing through a series of ridges and spurs of greater and greater altitudes until finally he attains the crest of the range; but on the east he passes at once from smooth, gently sloping treeless plains to a region of rugged peaks, glaciers, and waterfalls, with beautiful lakes nestling in all the valleys that head near the crest of the range.

Many persons conceive of a mountain chain as consisting of a single narrow ridge with steep slopes on both sides and a narrow, more or less regular serrate crest. Such a conception may be true of a few ranges, but generally a range is many miles in width and consists of a network of ridges and high spurs, some of which may be as prominent as the main watershed. The mountain range which crosses the Glacier National Park is of this character. It varies in width from 18 to 25 miles, and into this broad mass the streams on both sides have cut deeply, crowding the water parting or Continental Divide from one side to the other and forming a very irregular crest line. In fact, the mountain mass has been regarded by some writers as composed of two distinct ranges, the Lewis on the east and the Livingston on the west. The Continental Divide follows the crest of the Lewis Range from the southern boundary of the park to a point a short distance beyond Ahern Pass, and there it crosses to the summit of the Livingston Range.

The two mountain crests just described form a sort of rim around an area of comparatively level land known as Flattop Mountain, which stands at an altitude of about 6,500 feet. Although the Continental Divide lies along this mountain for a distance of about 20 miles, it is in effect a great topographic basin surrounded by a wall of mountain peaks from 1,000 to 4,000 feet above the general level. If the observer on one of the adjacent peaks could see in imagination the present valleys filled to a depth of 1,000 to 2,000 feet, he would then obtain a realistic picture of this basin as it must have been when it was formed, long before the present valleys were excavated. It was then, as now, a beautiful natural park with a rolling or undulating surface that stretched up to and blended with the slopes of the surrounding rocky rim. Some of the old gently rolling surface is still preserved on Flattop Mountain, covered by an open forest through which the traveler may ride at will and in which he can find nearly ideal camp sites, especially early in the season, when water is plentiful.

In other parts of the park the high peaks have no regular arrangement, except that they occur along the Continental Divide and on the spurs that project from both sides of it. The peaks rising more than 10,000 feet above sea level are Mount Cleveland, 10,438 feet; Mount Stimpson, 10,155 feet; Kintla Peak, 10,100 feet; Mount Jackson, 10,023 feet; and Mount Siyeh, 10,004 feet.

The most rugged topography is on the north and east sides of the high ridges and peaks, for the cirques cut by the present glaciers are more numerous on these sides and the ancient glaciers were much like those of the present day, except that they were more extensive and cut more deeply into the mountain mass. The difference in the appearance of the two sides of the mountains is striking, and the traveler can readily determine in which direction he is looking by the ruggedness or the smoothness of the slopes and crests he sees. If he looks north or east he sees generally rounded slopes and domelike crests, which seem to present little or no difficulty to the climber, and he might readily imagine that the reported ruggedness of the mountains had been greatly exaggerated, but if he turns about it becomes evident that on their opposite sides these apparently rounded crests are angular and precipitous and that in many places they are cut by cirques having nearly vertical walls which no climber can surmount and which give to the mountains a rugged grandeur that is seldom equaled.

Forests add greatly to the beauty of the park, for the trees grow only on the lower, more gentle slopes, forming a setting for the high peaks, which, by contrast, look much more rugged than they would were the surface entirely barren. The green mantle sweeps down with long, gentle curves to the bottoms of the valleys, in which nestle lakes ranging in size from mere ponds to sheets of water 9 or 10 miles in length and a mile or more in width. The lakes that are fed by glacial water are milk-white, but others are clear and pure and reflect all the varying aspects of the sky and clouds above. On a clear day the water is beautifully blue, but when storm clouds gather it assumes darker shades, which make it look dangerous and forbidding.

Of all the factors that add attractiveness and beauty to the park the streams are by no means the least. The clear, cold water glistens in the sunshine as it ripples over the variously colored pebbles in the bottoms of the streams or breaks in feathery torrents from the precipitous cliffs that abound on every hand.

ORIGIN OF THE TOPOGRAPHIC FORMS.

CONDITIONS WHEN THE ROCKS WERE LAID DOWN.

Although the mountain rocks are very, very old, they show by their form and composition that originally they were sediments laid down in water, either in large lakes or in the sea. The evidence of this origin consists principally of ripple marks, which were made by the waves when the material was soft sand along the beach, and of sun cracks and rain prints, which show that the mud of the bottom was from time to time exposed to the drying action of the air or to the storms that beat upon the coast. The presence of casts of salt crystals in some of the upper rocks seems to indicate that during at least part of the time the water was salt.

Most of the rocks were therefore deposited in a shallow sea or lake and consequently must have been nearly horizontal. As they are now far above sea level and not at all horizontal, it is manifest that great changes have occurred since they were laid down. It is impossible to say how many and what earth movements have taken place in this region, but the geologist is fairly certain that the movement which distorted the rocks and tilted them up at high angles was comparatively recent and that the movements which preceded this violent disturbance were merely broad uplifts or subsidences, which left the beds of rocks in much the same positions as those they originally occupied.

During each uplift the sea probably receded from this region, but it returned as soon as the land sank below the level of its surface. The last great inroad of the sea occurred at the time the rocks of the plains were being deposited. Then the waves swept across what is now the park, and no Front Range was in existence. Soon after that time, however, the sea was driven out by an uplift of the land, and the region has since been continuously above sea level. The traveler may wonder how many years have elapsed since that uplift, but the geologist must confess his inability to answer the question. He knows, however, that it has been a very long time—possibly several millions of years—and when in imagination one goes back in the history of the world several millions of years, it matters little whether he thinks of one million or twenty million, for both are inconceivable to human intelligence.

ROCKS UPLIFTED AND FAULTED.

Next came a time when all was movement and change. Deep-seated forces in the earth had been gathering energy until finally the stresses became so great that the rocky crust began to move. It is not definitely known what causes such stresses in the rocks. They may be produced by the shrinking of a slowly cooling globe; but be that as it may, there is positive evidence to show that after the rocks of the plains were laid down a great pressure developed in the mountain rocks, which caused them to tend to move toward the plains. The rocks of the plains were, however, immovable and as the stresses accumulated they found relief by the folding of the rocks. Here again is something just as inconceivable as the length of geologic time—the power necessary to move a great mass of rock thousands of feet in thickness and wrinkle it up as sheets of paper can be wrinkled in the hand. The geologist learns to accept such things without question, for although he may not be able to realize fully the forces involved in a movement of this sort the evidence of it is so plain as to be incontestable.

The probable results of the movement in the crust of the earth are shown in the accompanying diagram (fig. 1). Section A represents the edges of the rock strata in the condition in which they were originally laid down, before they had been deformed in any way. The force which affected them came apparently from the southwest, and as there was no escape from it, except by bending and wrinkling, it is supposed that one large fold and several small ones were produced, as shown in section B. The pressure, although slightly relieved by the corrugation, still persisted and the folds were greatly enlarged, as shown in section C. At this stage the folds had nearly reached their breaking limit, and when the pressure continued as time went on the strata broke in a number of places along the lines of least resistance, as indicated in the diagram, and the rocks on the west side of the folds were pushed upward and over the rocks on the east, as shown in section D. The mountain rocks (represented by patterns of cross lines) were shoved over the rocks of the plains (represented in white), producing an overthrust fault.

As the rocks on the west were thrust eastward and upward they made, in all probability, a greatly elevated region, but they did not at any time project into the air, as indicated in section D, because as soon as the rocky mass was uplifted above drainage level streams began to wear it away and to cut deep canyons in its upland portion, and they also reduced the soft rocks of the plains to a nearly even surface. The rocks of the mountains, owing to their more resistant character, still

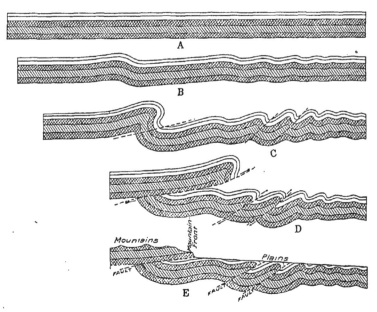

FIGURE 1.—Diagram illustrating manner in which the Lewis overthrust was produced and its effect on the aspect of the front range.

tower above the plains, and where they overlie the soft rocks the mountains are terminated by precipitous walls of limestone, as shown in section E. This explains the absence of foothills that is so conspicuous a feature of this mountain front and one in which it differs from most other ranges.

Naturally on these abrupt and exposed slopes the streams have cut deep gorges through the hard mountain rocks and down into the soft rocks of the plains, so that the actual trace of the fault on the surface is an irregular line zigzagging from spur to valley.

In places along the fault line the streams have cut through the overthrust mass, leaving isolated outliers of the hard mountain rocks far from the main line of the range. The most noted example of this kind is Chief Mountain, on the northeastern boundary of the park, which is formed of a single block of the mountain limestone completely isolated from other rocks of its kind and resting directly on the soft sandstone and shale of the plains. The mountain stands as a single monolith 1,500 feet high, facing the plains as if it were a sentinel standing guard over the hunting ground of the red man. The Indians called this mountain, from its commanding attitude, the "Old Chief," and it is still known by that name.

As shown on the map (Pl. XIII, in pocket), the fault separates the mountains from the plains along the east front throughout the extent of the park. It crosses the Great Northern Railway at Fielding, on the west side of the summit, and it passes into Canada where the North Fork of Belly River crosses the international boundary. Although it is present everywhere along the mountain front it is much more conspicuous in the northern than it is in the southern part of the park, because in the north the limestone which immediately overlies it is much thicker than it is in the south. In fact, at some places along the mountains just north of the railroad the limestone is lacking, and at other places it is so inconspicuous that it may not be noticed by the traveler if his attention is not directed to it.

Although the evidence regarding the presence and character of this fault is incontrovertible, there is still one question unanswered—How far has the overthrust mountain mass moved? To those who think of the "everlasting hills" as one of the immutable features of the earth such a question may seem startling indeed, but to the geologist it is the normal question, for to him all natural features are in a state of change, though the action is so slow that it is in most things imperceptible to the eye.

That the mountain mass of the park has been thrust far to the northeast from its original position, as illustrated by the diagram, is clearly shown, but the full extent of that movement may never be known, for it is difficult, if not impossible, to locate the place from which the mass was overthrust. Nevertheless, some idea of the extent of the movement may be obtained by measuring along the railroad the distance from the fault line where it crosses the valley at Fielding to the east boundary of the park, which agrees in a general way with the eastward extent of the overthrust mass. This distance is about 15 miles. Thus it is certain that the whole mass of rocky strata thousands of feet in thickness, weighing incredible millions of tons, has been shoved toward the northeast at least 15 miles, and were the original position of the mountain mass known the distance might prove to be much greater. On account of the great movement and the excellence of the exposures, this great fault, known to geologists as the Lewis overthrust, is destined to become a classic in geologic literature.

THE UPLIFTED MASS CARVED BY WATER.

Coincident with or consequent upon the overthrust came uplift of the region. This uplift stimulated all the streams to increased activity, and the great mass of the mountains was deeply scored by the canyons they cut. Running water is the most powerful agent known in carving mountains and other features of high relief. Where the streams have a sharp descent the cutting is rapid, but the force slowly becomes less effective as the grade is reduced, until the stream becomes sluggish, and then its cutting power ceases and it builds up instead of wearing down its channel. This process, which is known as erosion, may be witnessed by anyone in small rills or brooks after a hard rain. Each stream is swollen with water which, if the ground or rock over which the stream passes is soft, is heavily charged with mud and sand that act as cutting and scouring agents, effectively rasping the walls and deepening the channel of the stream. Where it reaches a lowland or pond the coarser sediment carried by the water is deposited, being spread out over the flat land or built out as a delta in a pond or lake.

The process of stream erosion may seem to many readers to be slow, but in reality it is rapid, for the streams, especially in a mountain country, are constantly charged with abrasive sand or gravel and so are always at work. There is no cessation, no relief from the endless rasping of the grains of sand on the beds of the streams, and as a result the hardest and most massive rocks are rapidly worn away. The streams cut deep gorges, which at first may have nearly vertical walls and be true canyons, but which in a region of considerable precipitation will sooner or later take on, in cross section, the form of a V.

As time goes on the streams cut farther and farther back into the mountain mass until they completely dissect it, leaving instead of an upland plateau a region of serrate ridges and sharp peaks. In this manner most of the mountains of the world have been produced— not by volcanic eruption and sudden movement but by gradual uplift and the dissection of the uplifted mass into rugged mountain forms by the streams.

It will be seen that the conspicuous features of the park are due to inequalities in the hardness and differences in the positions of the rock strata, which are composed of sediments originally laid down beneath the level of the sea, and to the work of water and ice acting on these uplifted strata. In this respect the Glacier National Park contrasts somewhat strongly with the Yellowstone National Park, where the most interesting features have resulted from volcanic phenomena and where water and ice have acted mainly on great lava flows and ash beds spread out from time to time on ancient land surfaces.

THE UPLIFTED MASS MODIFIED BY GLACIAL ICE.

Nearly all the valleys in the Glacier National Park show by their forms that they have been occupied by ice, although in many of them no glaciers exist at the present time. The form of a valley after it has been modified by moving ice is well illustrated by figure 2, **B**. It is known as a U-shaped valley, though the U may be very broad. Such valley forms could have been produced only by great masses of ice which filled the valleys to a depth of at least 2,500 feet and covered most of the lower slopes of the mountains. This of course means that immense glaciers must have originated in these mountains and moved out in all directions, extending 20 or 30 miles over the Great Plains on the east and down the valley of Flathead River on the west. The present glaciers are only the diminutive remnants of the earlier ones, and if the mean annual temperature were raised slightly

FIGURE 2.—Diagrams showing form of a stream-cut valley (A) and of the same valley after it has been occupied by a glacier (B).

or the amount of precipitation decreased they would probably disappear. As it is, they cling to the north and east sides of the high ridges and peaks, where the winter snows find a lodging place and where the summer sun has little effect upon them. There are no longer any great bodies of ice in this area, but the work they accomplished is still visible and lends beauty to the scenery, for the rugged mountain tops are accentuated by the rounded, graceful forms of the valley sides.

The glaciers have had an even more marked effect upon the topography than that of smoothing the valleys down which they extended. They had the power to cut into the mountain slopes at their heads, forming basins called cirques, which add greatly to the ruggedness and variety of the scenery. The process of cirque cutting is not well understood, but at or near the point where the névé or snow field changes into the moving ice of the glacier the cirque is formed. Blocks of rock are evidently plucked out by the ice, even back to the névé, and this tends to give to the cirque a nearly level floor. The effect of the backward plucking is to undermine the bordering walls, and these break down, giving to the excavation a circular or semi-circular form with nearly vertical walls from a few hundred to more than 3,000 feet in height.

The glaciers have not only produced the cirques, but are the direct cause of the formation of most of the lakes, large and small, which are without doubt one of the most attractive features of the region. Some of the lakes, such as McDermott, Red Eagle, Ellen Wilson, and Two Medicine, occupy rock basins that were scoured out by the old glaciers in places where the rocks were slightly softer than they were lower down the valleys. Such basins may be distinguished by the rocky barriers that cross them at the outlets. These ledges were not thrust up like dikes, as might perhaps be supposed. They have remained in their original positions, but the softer rocks farther up the valleys have been carried away, leaving basins in which the waters of the lakes accumulated.

Other lakes, such as Bowman and Upper Quartz, are held in place by great glacial moraines—accumulations of bowlders, mud, and other rock débris laid by the ice at the margin of the glacier—which have been deposited across their valleys like huge dams. Many of the small lakes and ponds also are rimmed about by moraines.

Lake basins of a third class have been produced by the glaciers, but in these the dam was not formed by a moraine, but by the outwash of sand and gravel from the end of the ice. The basins of Logging, Lower Kintla, Lower Two Medicine, and McDonald lakes are supposed to have been formed in this manner. At the extremities of these lakes there is no visible evidence of barriers, but the valleys below the lakes are filled deeply with coarse but well-rounded gravel which the streams flowing away from the ice carried and deposited, forming dams just as effectively as if moraines had been built around the ice front.

THE SURFACE FEATURES.

The foregoing pages contain a general description of the park and a brief outline of the various causes and conditions that have been instrumental in shaping its features. It has been shown that these processes are of the everyday kind and that the visitor to the park may see them in operation everywhere if he will only take the trouble to look.

An attempt will now be made to describe the most interesting features in each valley, not alone as things of beauty or interest to-day, but as forms resulting from past conditions. The history of the region is recorded in the topographic forms, and they are spread before us as an open book. Let us read them and not be content to pass them by unnoticed.

TWO MEDICINE VALLEY.

Two Medicine is the first valley in the park to be seen by the visitor who enters it at Glacier Park station. In fact, the station and hotel are within a few hundred yards of the main creek, but this part of the valley as well as Lower Two Medicine Lake lies outside of the park, and the scenic part of the valley is farther north.

Trails and camps.—The largest hotel connected with the park is that recently erected at Glacier Park station. From this hotel the traveler may go to the mountain valley of Two Medicine by the automobile road, or, if he prefers to travel in the "good old way," he can take the trail that keeps to the west of the lower lake and arrive at the same destination. Almost all visitors stop at a camp composed of log chalets at the foot of Two Medicine Lake, and from this camp the traveler can easily reach all parts of the valley that are now accessible. He can go up the north side of the lake by a trail which winds in and out through the timber and affords many beautiful views of the lake and of the high peak on the opposite side (Mount Rockwell) reflected in its placid waters. If he follows the trail, he will climb up through Bighorn basin, from which he may look back at the valley nestling at his feet and finally reach the Continental Divide at Dawson Pass. If he wishes to go in the other direction, he can proceed by a good trail up Paradise Creek and cross the range at Two Medicine Pass, or he can climb the east wall of the valley and enjoy the beauties of Buttercup Park just under Bearhead Mountain. Good camp sites, with wood and water in abundance and grass for saddle and pack animals, can be found at several places along Paradise Creek and also where the north trail leaves the valley floor and begins the ascent to Dawson Pass.

The form of the valley.—Two Medicine Valley is semicircular in cross section, just as it was left by the glacier which long ago occupied it and flowed far out on the plains to the east. The ice, in passing down the valley, scoured away most of the inequalities of its floor, but the great ledge of limestone that crosses it below the lake was too hard to be removed and in consequence remains as a barrier across the valley, through which the water has found an underground passage and now issues from a large hole and forms what is known as Trick Falls.

Lakes.—The portion of this valley within the park is occupied by two very interesting lakes, and a third lake that is somewhat less attractive lies just outside of the park boundary. The principal lake, by the side of which the camp is built, is a beautiful sheet of water bordered by grassy slopes or heavy timber. The basin in which it lies was scooped out of the relatively soft rock by the ancient glacier that occupied the valley.

Mountains.—Rising Wolf Mountain, the dominating feature of the valley, was named for one of the prominent chiefs of the Blackfeet

A. TWO MEDICINE VALLEY FROM SCENIC POINT, 2,100 FEET ABOVE THE LAKE.

Rising Wolf Mountain on the right, Appistoki Peak on the left, and Mount Rockwell in the center. Mount St. Nicholas is the distant peak just to the left of Mount Rockwell, and Mount Phillips is the left of Rising Wolf. Dawson Pass is visible to the right of Mount Phillips. Photograph by T. W. Stanton.

B. BELLY RIVER VALLEY FROM TRAIL A LITTLE EAST OF AHERN PASS.

Cirque wall at left 2,500 feet high. Lake Helen at base of wall but not visible. Elizabeth Lake in valley at the right. Peak of Mount Merritt just visible in left center. Unnamed glacier at the Photograph by T. W. Stanton.

A. "THE OLD SQUAW."

A huge block of argillite that has become separated from the main mass of Squaw
Mountain. Visible from the hotel at Glacier Park station. Photograph by
T. W. Stanton.

B. TRIPLE DIVIDE PEAK.

From this peak (marked A) the waters drain into the Gulf of Mexico, Hudson Bay, and the Pacific Ocean. Split
Mountain on the right and Norris Mountain in the center. On the far side both these mountains have vertical
walls more than 1,000 feet high. Photograph by T. W. Stanton.

Indians. The other noteworthy peaks are Mount Grizzly, a sharp pyramidal peak at the south end of the valley, and Mount Rockwell, towering above and almost overlooking the upper lake. The mountain, which is most conspicuous from the camp, is in reality only the end of a prominent spur of Mount Rockwell, but, on account of its commanding position, it seems to the traveler like a sentinel standing guard over the valley, which, now so peaceful, has been the scene of many encounters between the bands of Indians that frequented it as their hunting ground. The mountain is not so high as the main summit of Mount Rockwell, but it is much more prominent, as it stands 3,100 feet above the surface of the lake, and from its steep front and its nearness to the shore, it seems to overhang the water. The relation of the prominent peaks surrounding this valley is well shown in Plate II, *A*, which also shows something of the fine setting that these rugged peaks and wooded slopes provide for Two Medicine Lake.

Cirques.—Although no glaciers are to be found at the present time in Two Medicine Valley, glacial cirques are numerous, and they show that the ice of the old glaciers must have filled the valley to a great depth and also covered much of the surrounding mountain slopes. Every tributary of the creek heads in a cirque that has been rounded out and cut back by a glacier until in many places the bordering walls are nearly vertical. Astor, Buttercup, and Paradise parks, Bighorn Basin, and the basin of Upper Two Medicine Lake are all cirques, and there are many others that are equally interesting but not so well known. Most of these cirques were gouged out below the outer rocky rim, so to-day they hold lakes and ponds which add very much to their attractiveness.

Geologic features.—The geologic feature of most interest in the Two Medicine Valley is the Lewis overthrust fault, which marks the eastern base of the mountains and to which is due the abruptness of the slope along that front. The fault crosses the valley at the base of the limestone ledge through which plunges the water of Trick Falls and then swings outward, crossing the ridge on the north side of the valley at the base of the steep slope of Spot Mountain. To the south it also passes around the base of the limestone cliff at the point of the mountain and crosses Fortymile Creek at the place where the trail from Glacier Park station first approaches that stream. From Fortymile Creek the fault passes around the valley of Midvale Creek and then swings far out around the base of "The Old Squaw," a detached portion of Squaw Mountain (Pl. III, *A*), and so on around projecting spurs and into deep ravines to the park boundary at Fielding, far west of the Continental Divide.

From this fault the rocks dip gently toward the west, exposing first a mass of greenish argillite about 1,800 feet thick and then the very red argillite that makes the great bulk of Rising Wolf Mountain and gives to it its charming color. The highest rock, a yellowish limestone, is found in Flinsch Peak and Mount Morgan, at the head of Dry Fork.

CUT BANK VALLEY.

Cut Bank Valley lies next north of Two Medicine Valley. The creek draining it flows across the Blackfeet Indian Reservation, by the town of Cut Bank, and unites with Two Medicine Creek to form Marias River, so named in 1805 by Lewis and Clark in honor of a cousin of Capt. Clark. Marias River flows into Missouri River about 50 miles below Great Falls.

Trails and camps.—The automobile road from Glacier Park station crosses North Fork of Cut Bank Creek about 3 miles outside of the boundary line of the park, but, as shown on the map (Pl. XIII), a branch road leads up the valley to the Great Northern camp. Above this camp there is a good trail which follows the valley to its head and then by a climb of about 1,000 feet crosses the summit at Cut Bank Pass and descends into Nyack Valley on the west. Camping places where forage for animals is abundant are not numerous, but there are a few opposite Mount James, and late in the season, when the snow has disappeared, excellent sites can be found on the banks of some beautiful little lakes or ponds at the extreme head of the valley.

The form of the valley.—The valley of Cut Bank Creek is well rounded, showing that it was at one time occupied by a great glacier, which filled it to a depth of at least 2,000 feet. This vast body of ice moved down the valley, scouring off the irregularities of the rocky floor and broadening the bottom from the sharp V shape, characteristic of stream-cut valleys, to the form of a U. The glacier then moved for a long distance eastward upon the plain, overflowing its immediate banks in several places where they were low. One of these spillways can be seen in the north wall of the valley just beyond the park line, and others on both the north and south sides where the automobile road crosses the valley.

Mountains.—The mountains in this valley and on the bordering ridge are not particularly prominent. Mount James, which has on the north a very precipitous face about 1,800 feet high, is the most commanding, its summit being about 4,300 feet above the level of the camp. The most noted mountain in this vicinity is Triple Divide Peak, shown in Plate III, *B*, which is so named because the water falling on it goes in three directions—part flowing east down Cut Bank Creek and thence by way of Marias and Missouri rivers to the Gulf of Mexico; part flowing north down Red Eagle Creek and thence by St. Mary and Saskatchewan rivers to Hudson Bay; and part flowing west down Nyack Creek and by way of Flathead and Columbia rivers to the Pacific Ocean. This small peak may therefore be regarded, so far as drainage is concerned, as the culminating point of the continent. Mount Morgan, at the head of the valley, is also fairly conspicuous, especially to the traveler crossing Cut Bank Pass.

Glaciers.—Few glaciers can be found in this part of the park. The largest, a mass of ice about half a mile wide, lies on the north slope of Mount James. Two other small glaciers, not shown on the map, lie in the upper valley, one on the west side at a point where the Continental Divide leaves the immediate valley wall, and the other nearly opposite but not visible from the trail.

Cirques.—The old glacial cirques and cirque walls are not particularly prominent nor imposing in Cut Bank Valley, although every side ravine as well as the head of the main valley ends in such a feature. The reason for this inconspicuousness is that few of the cirques were cut back into the mountains far enough to leave vertical or even rugged and precipitous walls. As a rule the back walls of the cirques in this valley are steep for a height of 1,500 or 2,000 feet, but the slope is broken by few vertical faces. Probably the most imposing wall rises above the present glacier on Mount James and has a height of about 1,300 feet. The little glacier on the peak next north of Red Mountain is likewise bounded on the back by a rugged wall about 1,000 feet high. The small glacier on the west side of the valley lies in a cirque 700 feet deep with walls that are practically vertical. This cirque, although small, is an excellent example of such a feature and shows clearly how an amphitheater has been cut out of the solid rock by a small glacier which originally found a lodging place on a rocky shelf on the mountain side. The traveler who is interested in the formation of glacial cirques can easily reach this one from a camp at the head of the valley by climbing the trail to the pass and then continuing north along the summit until he finds himself on the margin of the cirque, from which he can look down at the little glacier that has accomplished so much work, lying in its rocky bed 700 feet below. He can then realize how steep are the walls and how the glacier has cut horizontally back from its original resting place.

Geologic features.—The geologic feature of greatest interest in this valley is the Lewis overthrust fault, which has controlled in large measure the development of the topography along the east front of the range. The position of the fault is well marked at the base of the yellow limestone cliff which can be seen on both sides of the valley from Cut Bank camp. It swings around from the base of the great cliff on the south and crosses the main stream nearly 2 miles above the camp. Here the limestone forms a distinct terrace which extends across the valley and in which the stream has cut a deep gorge. From the bottom of the gorge the fault rises and passes around the base of White Calf and Divide mountains and enters the valley to the west.

RED EAGLE VALLEY.

Red Eagle Valley lies west of the Hudson Bay Divide, and its waters, after uniting with those of St. Mary River, find an outlet into Saskatchewan River. The valley is short but is one of the most charming and picturesque in the park.

Trails.—There are no camps in this valley, although the automobile road from Glacier Park station enters its lower part and the hotel at St. Mary might be regarded as standing at its lower end. From St. Mary the Red Eagle trail passes through a broad, open upland in which grass is abundant and many excellent camp sites may be found, but beyond the place where the trail descends to the creek the valley is closely shut in by the mountains and the timber is very dense. Red Eagle Lake, although small, is visited by many travelers because of the good fishing it affords and also because of the beauty of the lake and the adjacent mountains. Beyond the lake the trail is very poor, and few persons have ascended to the head of the valley and crossed the Continental Divide to the Nyack Creek trail on the south. Camp sites and grazing can be found late in the season on the broad platform just under the summit, but below that place the forest is very dense down as far as Red Eagle Lake.

The form of the valley.—Red Eagle Valley is broad and open for a creek of its size. Its U-shaped cross section shows clearly that it has in times past been occupied by an immense glacier that scoured and rounded the original V-shaped valley cut by the stream. The north side of the Continental Divide at the head of Red Eagle Valley afforded a good gathering ground for the snow; hence Red Eagle Glacier at one time was probably 2,000 feet deep. This great body of ice broadened the valley bottom and steepened the walls, especially where exposed spurs projected into the valley. Thus the west face of Split Mountain and the spur opposite, as well as the east face of Red Eagle Mountain, have been scoured to a height of at least 2,000 feet, leaving smooth, nearly vertical mountain slopes.

Mountains.—Red Eagle and Split mountains are the most conspicuous peaks in the basin. The former is very rugged and precipitous, but the latter is more characteristic of the region, for, as its name indicates, the mountain appears to have been split as if a giant knife had severed it and removed the north half. In reality the north half has been removed by a glacier, the diminutive representative of which still lies at its foot. The peak as seen from the north resembles the gable end of a house, having a form that is very common in the high peaks of this region. Many other mountains in the basin are interesting, but as they present no striking features they will not be mentioned.

Glaciers.—Red Eagle Valley contains more glaciers than any of the valleys to the south, but even here there are no large ones. The most extensive is the Red Eagle Glacier, which stretches along the north side of the Continental Divide for about 2½ miles. It is not wide but in one place thrusts a long tongue of ice down the valley and is therefore representative of both the bench and the valley types of glaciers. The next most prominent glacier—prominent because it can be seen from almost any point in the valley below—is the one at the north foot of Split Mountain. Two small glaciers lie on the east side of Little Chief Mountain, two on the north side and under Norris Mountain, and one still farther west on the Continental Divide.

Cirques.—Red Eagle Valley is characterized by very finely developed cirques, some of which are nearly semicircular, though others are broad, irregular shelves cut in the northern or eastern slopes of the mountains. Many of them are bordered by steep slopes, but some have nearly vertical walls that stretch up to the summits of the mountains above. Probably the best-known cirque in this valley is that on Split Mountain. The glacier that carved it could never have been large, for the cirque merely "hangs" on the side of the main valley; nevertheless it has been cut deeply into the mountain and exhibits vertical walls nearly 1,700 feet high. The cirque wall on the north side of Norris Mountain is of about the same height but is not so steep. The wall back of Red Eagle Glacier is also imposing, being fully 1,200 feet high. One of the largest and most perfectly formed of the old cirques is that which lies about 1½ miles north of Mount James. It is nearly circular and has a diameter of about a mile and a half. It is cut deeply into a round mountain mass, producing a "half dome" suggestive of similar features in the Yosemite National Park of California. The wall on the northwest side of the dome is 1,900 feet high, and the upper 1,000 feet is practically vertical. The main head of the valley is a compound cirque, consisting of two basins separated by a rise of 700 or 800 feet. It is evident that Red Eagle Valley has been greatly modified by the ancient glaciers that nearly filled it and is also being modified by the small glaciers of to-day, which are slowly cutting into the mountain slopes.

Geologic features.—As in all the other valleys on the east side of the mountains, the great Lewis overthrust fault, which separates the hard rocks of the mountains from the soft rocks of the plains, is the dominating geologic feature of Red Eagle Valley. Its position on the spurs and on the valley floor is well marked by the base of the yellow limestone, which forms cliffs that are easily seen from almost any point in the valley. The fault swings round the base of Divide Mountain at an altitude of about 7,500 feet and round Kootenai Mountain at about 6,300 feet and gradually approaches the valley floor, which it crosses a little below Red Eagle Lake. It then rises slightly, passing around the point of the mountain toward Lake St. Mary at an altitude of 5,200 feet. The old glacier failed to cut away the heavy, resistant limestone lying just above the fault, but it succeeded in eroding the soft green argillite above, forming a rock-walled basin in which Red Eagle Lake now lies.

ST. MARY VALLEY.

St. Mary Valley is one of the largest valleys on the east side and contains a wealth of beautiful and greatly diversified scenery. At present it is the principal highway across the range and is probably seen by more travelers than any other part of the park. Sooner or later, however, other valleys will be made accessible by the building of roads or trails, and the traveler will find that they are fully as attractive as St. Mary Valley.

Trails and camps.—This valley contains a well-worn trail to Gunsight Pass, at an altitude of about 7,000 feet, beyond which the trail descends to Glacier Hotel, at the head of Lake McDonald. There is also a poor wagon road up the northwest side of St. Mary Lake as far as The Narrows, but good boat service can be had on the lake to save the traveler from the unpleasant experience of a trip over this road. Recently a trail has been constructed from the upper end of the lake across Piegan Pass to Swiftcurrent Valley, and as this trail makes accessible some of the finest scenery in the park it is destined to become very popular. At the foot of St. Mary Lake the Great Northern Railway has established a comfortable hotel, which is connected with Glacier Park station by an automobile road over which most travelers now find their way into the park. Camps composed of log chalets have been formed at The Narrows, on the lake, and also at the foot of Gunsight Lake, near the Continental Divide. From the Gunsight camp the traveler can easily reach the Blackfeet Glacier, which is the largest one in the Rocky Mountains in this country.

The form of the valley.—St. Mary Valley is generally broad and open for a mountain valley. Originally it was doubtless narrow and sharply V shaped, like most valleys that are carved by running water, but since it was so cut it has been occupied by ice, and great glaciers have issued from every tributary valley and ravine, swelling the main glacier into an enormous mass of ice fully 2,000 feet deep. This ice stream was joined by that flowing from Red Eagle Valley and eventually by those from Boulder, Swiftcurrent, and Kennedy valleys, on the north, making a vast field of ice that extended down St. Mary Valley as far as Babb, where it overflowed its banks and sent many ice tongues out over the prairies on the east. Where the rocks were soft the glacier scoured out a wide valley, but where they were hard the valley is narrower. Thus below The Narrows and also above the upper end of the lake the rocks are relatively soft and the valley is broad, but from The Narrows to the upper end of the lake the

ST. MARY LAKE AND RED EAGLE MOUNTAIN.

From north shore just below The Narrows.   Lewis overthrust fault at base of limestone cliff.   Photograph by
Kiser, furnished by Great Northern Railway.

rocks are much harder and here the valley is narrow, the rugged walls descending steeply to the margin of the water. The Narrows is due to the presence of a hard bed of limestone that crosses the valley at this place. In passing over it the glacier succeeded in cutting it down in the middle of the lake, but left two points projecting from the shores, which afford excellent building sites for cottages and camps.

Lakes.—The great charm of St. Mary Valley is the lake, which is hemmed in by high mountains on either side. (See Pl. IV.) It is one of the most beautiful sheets of water in the world, reflecting all the varying colors of the landscape, from the azure blue of the summer sky to the glowing red that tints the highest peaks as the sun sinks below the western horizon.

This valley was doubtless at one time occupied only by a stream that meandered over the rocky bottom, which had been smoothed and scoured by the ice of the great glacier. Into this valley Swift-current Creek poured a large amount of sand and gravel, building up a huge delta that finally extended entirely across the valley, effectively ponding the waters above. Thus a lake 16 miles long was produced; but other streams were at work carrying sand and gravel into the valley, and Divide Creek on the south and Wild Creek on the north also built out deltas, which finally coalesced, separating the body of water into the two lakes that exist to-day. The traveler can see these deltas spread out below him if he looks back from the trail as he climbs it on his way to Boulder Creek.

Gunsight Lake is a small but well-known lake at the head of the valley. The trail to Gunsight Pass climbs from a point near the lower end of the lake up the smooth, steep slope of Mount Jackson, attaining a height above the lake at its upper end of about 1,000 feet. From this commanding point the traveler's view of Gunsight Lake is unobstructed by even a rock or a tree, and he may wonder what would happen were he to miss his footing. An excellent view of the lake with Going-to-the-Sun Mountain as a background may be obtained from Gunsight Pass. Twin Lakes, north of Fusilade Mountain, and a small lake on Goat Mountain complete the list of lakes in St. Mary Valley.

Mountains.—Around St. Mary Valley are many imposing mountain peaks, either on the high rim that bounds it or on the spurs between the tributary streams. Mount Jackson is one of the higher peaks of the park, standing 10,023 feet above sea level, or 5,550 feet above St. Mary Lake. This mountain is seen by all travelers who cross Gunsight Pass, and the front it presents to the Blackfeet Glacier is long remembered on account of its deep-red color. Mount Siyeh is another high peak, reaching an altitude of 10,004 feet. Heretofore this mountain could be seen at close range only from the Canyon Creek valley, but with the completion of the trail across Piegan Pass the traveler can readily ascend the mountain and look down 4,200 feet at Cracker Lake, almost beneath his feet.

Fusilade Mountain is one of the great landmarks of St. Mary Valley. It stands like an obelisk at the head of the valley, dazzlingly bright in the sunshine or piercing the storm clouds as they roll over the summit of the Continental Divide. From The Narrows it is a commanding object, and it is shown in most pictures of the valley. The north side of the mountain is very precipitous, but the south slope is more gentle. Another peak that is equally prominent and decidedly more imposing is Going-to-the-Sun Mountain, which, like the prow of a huge battleship, towers a mile in the air above St. Mary Lake.

Many other peaks, as Goat, Reynolds, Citadel, Little Chief, and Red Eagle, stand along the rim of the valley and serve as a rugged setting for the beautiful lake that it contains.

Glaciers.—The Blackfeet Glacier, which lies in St. Mary Valley on the north side of the Continental Divide just east of Mount Jackson, is the largest and best-known glacier in the park. It is easily reached from Gunsight camp and has been visited by most travelers who have crossed the range by this route. The glacier is fully 3½ miles in width, but including Harrison and Pumpelly glaciers, which are really parts of the same great mass of ice, though separated by low ridges of the mountain crest, there is at least 5 miles of ice along the summit of the range. The Blackfeet Glacier is much broken up by cascades and consequently has numerous crevasses. The lower part of the glacier, particularly on the west side, extends down the valley in a long tongue of ice, which gives to the glacier its double type—a bench and also a valley glacier. It presents on a small scale the form and features of much larger glaciers in other parts of the world. It has built up around its lower end some good examples of moraines, which consist of the loose material carried down by the ice. This material is dropped wherever the ice melts, but it is all gathered together, pushed ahead, and piled in a high ridge when the glacier readvances.

Several small glaciers are visible from the trail over Gunsight Pass, and the traveler who essays this route early in the season is sure to find across the trail large snow banks which to his imagination may seem like real glaciers, but later in the summer these disappear and he may make the trip over an unobstructed pathway.

A small glacier lies far back in the cirque on the north side of Fusilade Mountain, one perches high on the side of Piegan Mountain, and another is found on the north side of Going-to-the-Sun Mountain not far from the St. Mary camp. The one last mentioned, which is known as Sexton Glacier, is seldom seen because it is so well concealed by the great mountain peak that stands between it and the valley.

Cirques.—In St. Mary Valley there are a number of cirques which are worthy of attention, some for the great height of their walls and some for the regularity of their outline. One of the most remarkably symmetrical cirques lies high on the side of Red Eagle Mountain and, although it is visible from St. Mary Lake, it is at so great an altitude and so far away that its true shape has probably been realized by few observers. Its circular walls are from 1,000 to 1,700 feet high and extend around three-quarters of the circumference of the cirque. Other circular amphitheaters lie at the heads of the three branches of Roes Creek, which flows into the lake in the vicinity of the camp at The Narrows. The cirque lying nearest to the camp contains a beautiful lake surrounded by a wall from 2,000 to 2,300 feet high. The other cirques are regular in outline but not so deep. The cirque northeast of Whitefish Mountain is remarkable in that it opens toward the southeast, and the glacier that formerly occupied it must have been exposed to the full effect of the sun's rays. Another cirque just below Siyeh Pass is even more remarkable, for it opens toward the afternoon sun, a direction not at all favorable for the formation of a glacier.

The cirque which is seen by most people, but always at a distance, is that on the north side of Fusilade Mountain. This has been cut into the range that forms the Continental Divide and on the south is bounded by a nearly vertical wall 2,700 feet high. In looking up the valley from the lake the traveler might easily imagine that Fusilade Mountain is like the "spire" of Mount Pelee and that it had been forced up by volcanic action. Such was not its origin, however, for the mountain peak is merely a remnant left by the cutting out of the cirque just mentioned. The great cirque in which Gunsight Lake lies is also well known, but here the walls, although high, may be described merely as steep and only in places precipitous.

Moraines.—There are no terminal moraines in St. Mary Valley, and the lateral moraines that are rather prominent in the lower part are outside of the park. The one that is the most easily seen by the traveler who follows the ordinary routes of travel is on the west side of the valley, on the trail from St. Mary to Swiftcurrent Valley. When he comes to the top of the hill on this trail, he will see on his right some sharp little hills capping the ridge parallel to the lake. These hills are composed of gravel and sand that were carried down by the glacier when it filled the valley to a depth of about 1,200 feet and were crowded to the side and dropped, forming a lateral moraine. A corresponding ridge is present on the opposite side of the valley, but here a part of the ice stream found an outlet to the right, through the basin now occupied by Duck Lake, and the lateral moraine bends toward the east and dies out on the irregular surface of the plain. Those who reach the park by way of Browning and

Babb can get a good view of this moraine as they cross it on the stage road south of Duck Lake. The main stream of the glacier continued down the valley across the line of the international boundary and in a number of places built lateral moraines, but these are far beyond the ordinary lines of travel and hence will not be described.

Geologic features.—The Lewis overthrust fault has played a prominent part in controlling the mountain features of this valley, especially of the lower part. If it were not for this fault and the heavy resistant limestone that adjoins it there would be no narrows in the lake and no cliffs around Singleshot and Flattop mountains. The fault swings in from Red Eagle Valley, crosses the lake just below The Narrows, and rises rapidly, skirting the foot of the limestone cliff around Singleshot and Flattop mountains. On the extreme point of Flattop the wall of limestone and argillite on the upper side of the fault is 700 or 800 feet high and practically vertical.

Mining.—The town of St. Mary, consisting of about a dozen log cabins, was established a number of years ago as the result of a "gold rush." Gold was reported in the sand and gravel of Divide Creek and many people flocked to the camp, but the rumor proved to be without foundation and the camp was abandoned. The indications of copper ore, which at an earlier date caused the excitement that led to the purchase from the Indians of all the land east of the summit, occur mainly along a zone in which faults and dikes of igneous rock cut the limestone and argillite. This mineralized zone extends from White Calf and Divide mountains across Kootenai Mountain, the valley of St. Mary, and the heads of Boulder and Swiftcurrent creeks. Prospecting has been carried on all along this zone, but with indifferent success, as little ore has been found. Here and there the traveler, if he is a good mountain climber, will come upon the old pits and cabins of the prospectors, the last remaining mementos of the mineral boom that brought this country to the attention of the public and eventually led to the creation of the park.

BOULDER VALLEY.

Boulder Creek, lying between St. Mary River and Swiftcurrent Creek, flows in a small valley that offers little attraction to the traveler in search of picturesque scenery, although here and there beautiful views can be obtained. It has the distinction of having had at one time a wagon road nearly to its head, but lack of use and repairs has rendered this road difficult to travel, even for a pack train. It can be reached by a trail across the hills from St. Mary Valley and also from the Sherburne lakes in Swiftcurrent Valley. Boulder Valley is generally open and has little timber to interfere either with the view or with the grazing of animals. For the traveler who desires rest and good fishing this valley might prove to be an attractive resort.

There are few prominent peaks in this drainage basin. The most conspicuous landmark is Point Mountain, between Boulder and Swiftcurrent creeks. The base of the cliff on the front of this mountain can easily be reached from an old trail that crosses the low ridge about a mile to the northeast.

Every side ravine entering the valley is terminated at its head by a partly or completely developed cirque, but the best example is that at the head of the valley. This cirque is compound, a small one lying 500 feet above the principal one, and 100 feet still higher is the flat Siyeh Pass, which probably represents the union of two cirques on opposite sides of the ridge separating Boulder Creek from the headwaters of St. Mary River.

The Lewis overthrust fault is well shown in Boulder Valley and the yellow limestone on the upper side is much thicker here than it is farther south, making very prominent cliffs. The fault enters the valley from the extreme point of Flattop Mountain, skirting the base of the cliff on the south but gradually descending until it crosses Boulder Creek about 3 miles above Point Mountain. It then rises slightly and passes around Point Mountain at the bottom of the great limestone cliff, which has a height of nearly 1,000 feet. In places the limestone is broken by a number of small faults, which cause displacements of about 100 feet. These small faults occur in the same zone that is marked by dikes and faults in St. Mary Valley. Traces of copper ore have been found along this zone and many prospect pits have been dug without finding sufficient ore to pay for mining.

From time to time there has been considerable excitement on the subject of oil in the park, and two wells have been drilled on Boulder Creek, but like the copper prospects they were not successful.

SWIFTCURRENT VALLEY.

The valley of Swiftcurrent Creek is one of the best known valleys of the park. It has been famous in the mining history of the region and, at the height of the excitement, it was the principal avenue through which supplies were taken westward into the mountains. It is noted for the beauty of its scenery and, on account of its accessibility, it was visited by a great many people even before the creation of the Glacier National Park.

Trails and camps.—At the time of the copper excitement, several years ago, work was started on a claim on Cracker Lake, at the head of Canyon Creek. A mill was erected and elaborate preparations were made to mine the ore on a large scale. A wagon road was built to the workings and a typical western mining camp sprang into existence at the old town of Altyn, situated where Canyon Creek joins Swiftcurrent Creek. The hopes of the owners evidently failed of realization, but the wagon road from Babb to Altyn remains as a monument to their faith in the undertaking. The part of the road leading up Canyon Creek has been washed away and is now only a second-class trail.

The copper prospectors on Mineral Creek, on the opposite side of the range, built a very good trail up Swiftcurrent Creek and across Swiftcurrent Pass as a highway by which supplies could be brought into their camps from the outside world. (See Pl. V, *B*.) A poor trail up the north fork of the creek leads to Iceberg Lake, one of the most exquisite little lakes in the park. Recently a new trail has been completed across Piegan Pass, giving this valley a much-needed mountain connection with the upper end of Lake St. Mary.

The Great Northern Railway has established a camp of several log chalets at the lower end of Lake McDermott, from which all the points of greatest interest can be easily reached.

The valley of Swiftcurrent Creek below Lake McDermott is a broad, open plain in which grass was originally very abundant but has recently been exhausted by the large number of horses required for the use of travelers. Some pasture and a camp site can be found on the trail to Iceberg Lake, but the ideal spot in which to camp is the open grassy stretch just in front of that lake. There is also some grazing to be had up the main valley, but almost all parties going in that direction press on across the pass so as to stop in the ideal camp ground of Granite Park.

The form of the valley.—All the tributary valleys of Swiftcurrent Valley give evidence by their shape and by the smoothness of their sides of having been scoured out by the great glacier which in times long past moved out from the Continental Divide and mingled with the great ice stream coming down St. Mary Valley. In the hard rocks of the mountains the valleys are of ordinary size, but as soon as the ice struck the soft rocks of the plains about Altyn it carved a broad valley with gently rounded slopes. Much of the material carried down by the present stream has been dumped into the deeper St. Mary Valley in the vicinity of Babb, damming back the water and forming the lakes which are so attractive a feature of that valley.

Lakes.—Swiftcurrent Valley contains lakes which, though small, are justly renowned for their beauty. The most noted of these are Lake McDermott, upon which the camp is located, and Iceberg Lake, at the head of the North Fork. There is a very attractive group of lakes in Cataract Canyon. The middle lake of this group in particular is a fine body of water as seen from the trail that leads to the old Josephine mine, on the point of Grinnell Mountain. These lakes are by the side of the trail that leads to Grinnell Glacier and is now extended across Piegan Pass. The main Swiftcurrent Valley contains a string of small lakes or ponds, which, though mostly shallow and uninteresting when seen at close range, appear as emerald pools when

A. SWIFTCURRENT VALLEY, WITH McDERMOTT LAKE IN THE FOREGROUND.

Grinnell Mountain at the right and Mount Gould at the left. Lake held in place by the great limestone barrier
that crosses the valley in the foreground. Photograph by T. W. Stanton.

B. PACK TRAIN CROSSING A SNOWBANK ON THE SWIFTCURRENT TRAIL.

Photograph by R. H. Chapman.

A. LOWER END OF GRINNELL GLACIER.

Mount Gould in the background.   Band of dark diorite showing halfway
up the slope of the mountain.   Lateral moraine piled up by the glacier
in the foreground.   Photograph by T. W. Stanton.

B. AVALANCHE LAKE.

Dense forest coming down to the water's edge.   Heavens Peak in the background at the right and Mount Vaught
at the left.   Photograph by Bailey Willis.

viewed from the heights above. They are hemmed in by a dense forest, which, as seen from above, looks like a thick green carpet covering the valley bottom and all the lower mountain slopes. Farther down are the Sherburne Lakes, but they are so far away that they can claim the mountains only as a distant background. All these lakes reflect the ever-shifting panorama of the clouds and mountains, and their color changes with each variation in the tint and texture of the objects they reflect.

Mountains.—Three peaks are always associated in the mind of the traveler with this beautiful valley. These are Mounts Gould, Grinnell, and Wilbur. One of the most charming views in the whole park is that of Mount Gould from Lake McDermott, or from the next lake up Cataract Canyon. The mountain towers like the gable end of a huge building 4,700 feet above the level of the lake. (See Pl. V, *A*.) Grinnell Mountain is an imposing object from any point on the shore of Lake McDermott or farther down the valley, but it is not so awe-inspiring as Mount Gould. Mount Wilbur also looms high above the camp at Lake McDermott, a slender peak which stands in solitary grandeur, disdaining the companionship of its distant neighbors.

Mount Siyeh is very commanding as seen from Canyon Creek, for its summit seems to pierce the clouds as it stands 4,200 feet above the little lake that nestles at its foot. This peak, which attains a height of 10,004 feet, is the highest mountain associated with Swiftcurrent Valley.

Glaciers.—The largest body of ice in Swiftcurrent Valley is Grinnell Glacier (Pl. VI, *A*), which lies in a broad cirque at the foot of Mount Gould. It is a little more than a mile wide and it is rimmed for a distance of 2 miles by the steep fronts of Mount Gould and The Garden Wall. The latter stands about vertical and towers 1,000 to 1,500 feet above the ice. The traveler can reach the glacier by a climb of 1,200 feet from Grinnell Lake, or he can approach it from Granite Park by a climb of 1,000 feet over the Continental Divide at its back.

At the head of the main valley there are several glaciers that can be seen to good advantage from the Swiftcurrent trail. The glacier just south of the pass is spread out before the traveler as he climbs the steep part of the trail, and involuntarily he pauses in his climb to see the ice push forward over the edge of the shelf upon which it lies and go crashing to the bottom, some 1,500 feet below, but notwithstanding the fact that the ice comes to the very edge of the cliff and seems to overhang, no one has yet been fortunate enough to see it fall. This glacier is about three-quarters of a mile wide and extends back to the Continental Divide. The drainage of the glacier is very interesting. Most of it flows under the ice and falls headlong down the wall of the great cirque below, but some of the water finds a channel in the limestone underlying the glacier and discharges into Granite Park, on the other side of the Continental Divide. Thus the glacier, although lying on the Atlantic side, really sends part of its waters to the Pacific Ocean.

Three small glaciers lie on shelves on the mountain side north of Swiftcurrent Pass, but owing to a projecting mountain spur they are not visible from the trail except in the bottom of the valley. Two other glaciers are seen by many travelers, one lying just back of Cracker Lake and the other back of Iceberg Lake. The former does not descend to the lake level, but the latter forms a pretty picture as it gives off bergs of white ice that float in the indigo-blue water of the lake.

Cirques:—Swiftcurrent Valley contains many beautiful cirques, some of which still hold remnants of the glaciers that carved them, though most of the large ones have no sign of ice in their gigantic bowls.

Probably the most famous cirque in the park is that which holds Iceberg Lake. The glacier now occupying it has cut so far back into the mountain ridge that to-day the walls border the cirque for about three-quarters of its circumference. The walls are very high and steep—almost vertical. Four buildings like New York's great skyscraper, the Woolworth, placed one on top of another, would just reach from the surface of the lake to the highest point on the summit of the wall.

The great cirque that holds Grinnell Glacier, which has already been described, lies above another one, 1,200 feet lower, that furnishes a resting place for Grinnell Lake. The cirque at the head of Canyon Creek is one of the most remarkable in the valley. It holds Cracker Lake in its bottom, and its southern wall rises to the summit of Mount Siyeh, 4,200 feet above. The old glacier has eaten so deeply into the mountain that it has removed the north side, leaving the south half with a sheer vertical wall, as if some giant had cleft the mountain asunder and carried half of it away as a memento of his visit.

Cirques abound on every side. They make on the mind of the observer a contradictory impression; by their rounded outlines they tend to remove any suggestion of angularity from the surface features, but, on the other hand, by their great vertical walls they seem to add to the ruggedness of the region.

Geologic features.—The Lewis overthrust fault is without doubt the most striking geologic feature of this valley, and it is even more pronounced here than it is farther south. This difference is due to the fact that the limestone just above the fault is thicker here, and consequently the cliffs and precipitous slopes above the fault are stronger and present a sharper contrast with the rounded topographic forms of the shale below.

The fault is sharply outlined at the foot of the cliff on Point Mountain and also on Allen Mountain, west of Canyon Creek. It crosses Swiftcurrent Creek at the foot of the great ledge of limestone over which the water of Lake McDermott finds an outlet in a series of cascades and falls. From the deep pool below the falls the fault rises on the north wall of the valley, everywhere marked by the base of the great cliff of limestone, until it crosses the crest of the ridge and passes into the valley of Kennedy Creek.

The rocks about Lake McDermott show a pleasing variety of color. The outermost points of the spurs are composed of a limestone that gives to them a soft yellowish color; above this is an argillite that tinges the next succeeding points with green; and beyond these is a thick mass of bright-red argillite that makes a broad band of brilliant color. Grinnell Mountain, composed of this argillite, is a particularly striking feature. In some lights the red rock merely gives a rosy tinge to the yellow sunlight, but in others the mountain shows a deep-red color, as if it had been bathed in blood.

Another feature of geologic interest is a narrow band of dark rock that crosses the front of Mount Gould, as shown in Plate VI, A, passes under Grinnell Glacier, and reappears in Grinnell Mountain, everywhere forming a black band that is easily followed by the unaided eye. This dark rock, which is called diabase, was forced in a molten condition between layers of other rock. Generally it follows the bedding planes of the rocks, but in places it cuts through them as a great dike. Such a dike can be seen on the steep part of the Swiftcurrent trail. The band of diabase is visible on the north in the crest of Mount Wilbur and in the ragged wall surrounding Iceberg Lake.

The diabase should not be confused with another band of dark rock which lies higher on the mountain and shows on both sides of the trail in Swiftcurrent Pass and at other places on the Continental Divide. This rock, by its porous texture and ropy appearance, shows clearly that it was once a sheet of lava that was poured out on the bottom of the shallow sea or lake when the mountain rocks were being formed and that since that time it has been uplifted and folded with the inclosing rocks.

Mining.—The zone of fracture mentioned in the descriptions of the valleys lying farther south crosses Swiftcurrent Valley, passing through Allen Mountain, the point of Grinnell Mountain, Mount Wilbur, and Ahern Pass. At all these places prospects have been opened and some copper ore has been found, but nowhere has it been mined in sufficient quantity to pay for operation. There also has been considerable excitement regarding oil in this valley, and a number of wells have been sunk in the vicinity of the Sherburne Lakes, but though gas has been obtained in very small quantities nothing has been found that would justify the expense of drilling.

KENNEDY VALLEY.

The valley of South Fork of Kennedy Creek is open and fairly easy of access. A trail leads up the creek from a point beyond the boundary of the park, climbs the limestone wall at the entrance to the mountains, and passes round a little lake that lies behind this barrier and into the open valley beyond. The features of the valley that are of special interest are the steep north wall of a peak 1½ miles southwest of Appekunny Mountain and the limestone cliff and attendant fault that cross the valley below the lower lake. The former overlooks a fine example of a well-developed cirque, holding at its bottom Kennedy Lake, a small but beautiful sheet of water. The wall behind the lake is almost vertical and is about 1,800 feet high. The limestone cliff that overlies the fault and is conspicuous on the south side of the valley several miles below Kennedy Lake forms a barrier across the bottom, holding back the other lake. From this place it climbs the wall on the north, terminating in Sherburne Peak of Yellow Mountain, just outside of the park.

The traveler can enter the valley of North Fork of Kennedy Creek by a good trail which branches from the main wagon road just beyond Kennedy Creek, north of Babb. The trail was built to a prospector's camp on the main head of the stream, but it is reported that a very old and poor trail continues up to the summit of Seward Mountain. At one time there was a fairly good trail extending from the North Fork trail across the ridge west of Chief Mountain, but of late years it has been little used and now is almost impassable on the farther side of the ridge. The little lake lying just above the point where this trail leaves the North Fork trail, is most interesting, as it has been formed since the first edition of the topographic map was issued. A few years ago there were some cloudbursts on the east side of the mountains which caused all the streams to do great damage to their banks and flood plains. The water softened the shale on the slope south of the creek and a great mass slid down, blocking the valley and forming the lake.

Perhaps the feature that has added most to the charm of the valley of North Fork of Kennedy Creek is the great fault, which, although not visible to the eye, has been the controlling factor in the production of the most striking surface forms. The fault enters the valley at the foot of the great limestone cliff of Sherburne Peak. It follows the base of Yellow Mountain and crosses the valley floor just above the lake. From this point it rises to the summit of the ridge on the north at the point where it is crossed by the old trail and there swings back to the west into the valley of Belly River. The limestone lying just above the fault is very prominent here, as its thickness has been greatly increased during the process of faulting. When the mountain mass was moving toward the plains, as explained on page 10, the friction in places was so great that the limestone could not be pushed farther, the rocks broke again, and another layer of the limestone was shoved over the one in place. In Yellow Mountain the limestone has been thus broken and piled up five or six times, as it has also at the base of Chief Mountain, as shown in the accompanying diagram (fig. 3).

Long ago the hard mountain rocks extended continuously out along the ridge north of North Fork of Kennedy Creek to Chief Mountain, but the streams have been so active that they have cut it away, leaving only remnants here and there to mark its former position. Chief Mountain, the largest of these remnants, stands in massive grandeur overlooking more than 100 miles of plain to the east. The Indians recognized its resemblance to an old warrior and always referred to the mountain as "The Old Chief," and this name still clings to it. The mountain consists of a single block of limestone 1,500 feet high, with a front so nearly vertical that it can not be climbed, but the back slope is less precipitous and affords a route to the summit. The great fault cuts the mountain at its base. The rocks lying above the fault are very

FIGURE 3.—Diagram showing structure of Chief Mountain. Limestone in upper part not disturbed, but that in lower part duplicated by many minor oblique thrust faults. After Bailey Willis.

old, but the dark shale below is very young. This relation shows that the rocks of the mountains have been thrust toward the northeast, far out over the rocks of the plains, and that Chief Mountain represents a remnant of the overthrust mass.

Considerable prospecting has been done in this valley and some copper ore has been found, but not enough to justify the Government in passing title to the land, and so all the mineral claims have lapsed.

BELLY RIVER VALLEY.

The Belly River valley, though containing some of the most interesting scenery in the park, lies so far out of the range of ordinary travel that it has been visited by few persons and is comparatively unknown. On account of its many charming lakes and its high rugged mountains, however, it is destined, as soon as better lines of communication are established, to become one of the most frequented portions of the mountain region.

Trails.—The principal reason why this valley has not been visited is because the supposed horse trail leading into it from its head is not passable. This route was first used in 1890 by Lieut. George P. Ahern, then stationed at Fort Shaw, on Sun River. He was ordered to explore the mountain passes north of Marias Pass and accordingly, in company with Prof. G. E. Culver, of the University of Wisconsin, and a company of packers and soldiers from the fort, he visited Cut Bank and Swiftcurrent passes and after passing around the north base of Chief Mountain entered the valley of Belly River. He spent two days making a trail at the head of the valley and on August 22 took his entire outfit safely through the pass that bears his name. The only other man who has successfully traveled over this trail with pack horses is R. H. Sargent, of the United States Geological Survey. Since his trip several persons have attempted to take horses over this route, but they have learned to their sorrow that it can not be done in the present condition of the trail.

The only route by which the traveler can safely enter the valley at the present time is through the open plains country north of Chief Mountain. When once in the valley he can ascend the main stream as far as Helen Lake, or he can go up the Middle Fork to Glenns Lake. Plenty of grass can be obtained in the lower part of the valley, but in the mountains the valleys are in general heavily timbered and grass is scarce.

The form of the valley.—The Belly River valley has been broadened and smoothed by the great streams of ice that formerly occupied it and pushed far out upon the Canadian plains. The main or easternmost valley in particular, as shown in Plate II, *B*, has been scoured out until it has considerable breadth, but the Middle Fork valley is narrow, the slopes rising steeply from the margins of the lakes. Outside of the mountains the valley is like that of Swiftcurrent Creek, and its breadth is due to the softness of the rocks in which it has been cut.

Lakes.—This valley contains many lakes from which can be obtained magnificent views of the encircling mountains and the soft green slopes that lead down to the water's edge. Elizabeth, Crossley, and Glenns lakes lie in the broad, open valley, but all the rest occupy cirques cut down to the level of the valley floor or perched along the mountain sides. Helen, Margaret, and Sue lakes are each worthy of a visit; they are difficult to reach but can be seen from above by anyone who climbs the summit ridge from the Flattop side. In fact, no more impressive view can be obtained than that from the crest of the Continental Divide back of Sue Lake (Pl. VII, *A*). The panorama there unrolled will well repay the effort, as it requires a climb of only 500 feet from the Waterton Lake trail. The view from the north end of Crossley Lake is also one never to be forgotten, and the lover of nature who sees it will feel well repaid for the trouble and inconvenience he has incurred in forsaking the more accessible paths.

A. VIEW FROM CONTINENTAL DIVIDE JUST BACK OF SUE LAKE.

Mount Cleveland on the left; Mount Merritt on the right; valley of Middle Fork of Belly River in the center. Photograph by M. R. Campbell.

B. MOUNTAIN FRONT A LITTLE NORTH OF THE CANADIAN LINE.

ing abrupt change from plains in Belly River Valley. The peak in the center is at the extreme north end of the Lewis Range. The great fault cuts this range at the level of the plain. Photograph taken early in September by W. C. Alden.

Mountains.—On the margins of the Belly River valley are two very conspicuous mountain peaks—Mount Cleveland, 10,438 feet above sea level, the highest summit in the park, and Mount Merritt, 9,944 feet, one of the most rugged and isolated peaks of the region. Both of these peaks are prominent as seen from the summit above Sue Lake or from any point on the Continental Divide to the east within 3 miles. On a clear day they are sharply outlined against the deep-blue sky, but in stormy weather the clouds hover round their summits, sending off to leeward long streamers that are constantly being dissipated at the outer ends but as constantly renewed by the vapor that condenses around the peaks. Another mountain worthy of note is the fine pyramidal peak just northeast of Sue Lake. Although appearing insignificant from the platform in front of Chaney Glacier, this peak is very imposing when seen from Glenns and Crossley lakes, and the combination of the sharp, rugged peak and the snow-white Shepard Glacier, reflected in the shimmering waters of the lakes, is one that will linger long in the memory of the visitor who is fortunate enough to see it.

Glaciers.—The drainage basin of Belly River contains no large glaciers, but there are 18 medium-sized and small ones in different parts of it. Those along the Continental Divide are probably the best known, but only two of them, Chaney and Shepard, have been named. A large glacier lies just north of Ahern Pass and three or four cluster around the east face and north end of Mount Merritt. The location of the glaciers in this basin is typical of their arrangement throughout the park, for they are found only on the east and north sides of the ridges and peaks, the localities where the snow is most likely to find a lodging place and is best protected from the heat of the sun.

The traveler who visits Ahern Pass can easily reach the little glacier lying just over the summit on the northeast side. In fact, the trail to Helen Lake passes across the ice and he can examine all parts of the glacier without danger of any kind. Although this glacier is small, it has all the typical features of a bench glacier, including a well-developed moraine at its lower end. The traveler also, by a climb of about 1,500 feet from the trail at the head of Mineral Creek, can reach Chaney Glacier, which is about a mile in width and exhibits many interesting features. After examining the glacier he can easily tramp to the edge of the great cirque in front of the glacier and obtain a charming view down the valley, in which Margaret Lake lies 1,700 feet almost directly below.

Cirques.—Cirques abound in this basin, giving it an exceedingly rugged appearance. As the present glaciers are situated on the protected sides of the ridges and peaks, so also were the ancient glaciers, and hence all the cirques that they carved are found in such positions. The west side of a ridge, as Mount Merritt, may be perfectly smooth and uniform, but the east side is cut into most fantastic shapes and abounds in vertical walls which impart to it a most forbidding appearance. Thus, the cirque occupied by Helen Lake has walls about 2,500 feet high and that on the east face of Mount Cleveland has walls at least 3,000 feet high. The cirques are the dominant features of the topography, and the visitor can but wonder how the glaciers carved them out. The character of the rock apparently has had little effect on the work of the ice, the hard limestone and quartzite being removed as readily as the softer shale and argillite. Also, it has mattered little whether the rocks were horizontal or highly inclined. The power of the glacier seems to have been irresistible and its work was terminated only by the melting of the ice.

Geologic features.—The striking feature of the mountain front in this valley is the Lewis overthrust fault, which bears in from the base of the cliff on Chief Mountain, crossing the main fork of Belly River less than a mile below Elizabeth Lake. It crosses the Middle Fork just below Crossley Lake and then swings north around the spur between the Middle and North forks. It crosses the North Fork about 1½ miles above the park line and then disappears into Canada, crossing the international boundary at the foot of the limestone cliff a little west of the river. Everywhere along this fault line the limestone forms cliffs like great retaining walls, separating the mountains from the plains and giving to the front an abruptness that is very striking. (See Pl. VII, *B*.)

LITTLE KOOTENAI VALLEY.

The valley of Little Kootenai Creek, as shown on the map, appears to be in the heart of the mountains, but in reality the Lewis Range, which borders it on the east, terminates only a few miles north of the international boundary. Little Kootenai Creek flows around the end of the range and empties into Belly River and its valley opens directly on the plains to the east.

Trails.—The principal camping place in the valley is at the head of Waterton Lake, where grass is fairly abundant and all other requisites for a good camp site can be found. From this place the main trail ascends the valley for a distance of 6 miles and then climbs the slope on the east, crosses Flattop Mountain, and goes down McDonald Creek to the south. Another good trail turns westward up Olson Creek, crosses Brown Pass, and descends on the other side to Bowman Lake. A third trail follows the west shore of Waterton Lake across the international boundary to the post office of Waterton Mills, at the lower end of the lake. The trail is excellent on the United States side, but in Canada it is steep and rocky. Near the lower end of the lake there is a small hotel, from which travelers can enter the park by motor boat much more easily than they can by the trail.   In addition to the principal trails described above, there is a trail for 4 or 5 miles up Boundary Creek, but as it leads to no other valley it is not much used.   An old trail also extends up to the extreme head of the main valley, where it forks, one branch leading to West Flattop Mountain and the other crossing the ridge on the north to a small lake at the head of the South Fork of Valentine Creek, and then passing through open timber to Jefferson Pass.   The country in this vicinity is very beautiful, the woodlands containing many open, grassy glades which afford excellent pasture and sites for camps. Pasture can also be found in the valley at the head of Little Kootenai Creek, on Olson Creek, and on the summit of Brown Pass.

The form of the valley.—This drainage basin has been intensely glaciated and all the streams in it are flowing in flat-bottomed valleys. A notable feature is the unsymmetrical development of the side valleys, especially those joining the main valley from the west.   In each of these side valleys the north wall is smooth and regular and the divide on the north is much nearer the stream than that on the south.   This arrangement is doubtless due to the presence of glaciers and glacial cirques on the north side of the dividing ridge and their absence on the south side of the same ridge.   This unsymmetrical development makes the appearance of the country when viewed from the north very different from that which it presents when viewed from the south, and the observant traveler can soon learn to tell the points of the compass by the character of the landscape.

Lakes.—Waterton Lake is the principal body of water in this valley.   The upper half of the lake lies in the United States and the lower half in Canada.   It is hemmed in on all sides except the north by high mountains, which furnish the setting needed to bring out its beauties.   There are also a number of small lakes in the basin, of which those in Olson and Boundary valleys are the most noteworthy.

Mountains.—The highest peak in the vicinity of this drainage basin is Mount Cleveland, which has an altitude of 10,438 feet.   As seen from the west shore of Waterton Lake it is very imposing, but even there few persons realize that to gain its summit requires a climb of more than 6,000 feet.   The ascent can be most easily made from the ranger cabin just east of Citadel Peaks by a trail that leads well up toward the limit of heavy timber.   Although no other peak on the east side of the valley is so high as Mount Cleveland, the entire ridge is narrow crested and serrate and when seen from the head of Waterton Lake or from Jefferson Pass appears to be rugged in the extreme.   Good views of the picturesque mountain tops can be had from the summits on either side of Brown Pass, and these points of vantage can be attained by relatively short climbs.

Glaciers.—Few of the glaciers of this valley have received names, not so much because of their small size as because the region has until recently been almost inaccessible and its interesting features are little known. From a camp in Brown Pass the traveler can easily reach the glacier on the south side; in fact, he can camp nearly under the glacier and a short climb will take him to its foot. Similarly from a camp in Jefferson Pass the Carter Glaciers can be visited with but. little effort, and from the Continental Divide a little farther south the traveler can obtain an excellent view of the great Rainbow Glacier, high on the side of Rainbow Peak. This glacier is practically inaccessible from this direction, and the view just mentioned is the best that can be obtained. From the same viewpoint several of the glaciers on the north side of Vulture Peak are visible. One small glacier a little farther south but still high on the slope of the peak has the distinction of draining into both the Pacific and the Atlantic and consequently is known as the Two Ocean Glacier.

Cirques.—Like all the valleys already described, this one is marked by many imposing cirques, which add greatly to the rugged beauty of the landscape. Possibly the largest cirque here is that on the northwest side of Mount Cleveland, which as seen from Waterton Lake looks as if a great bite had been taken out of the side of the mountain by some gigantic animal. Its back wall is over 4,000 feet high, and the upper part is nearly vertical. The great cirque on the north face of Goathaunt Mountain has a back wall at least 2,000 feet high, the upper 1,200 feet of which, as shown by Plate VIII, is vertical. A very symmetrical cirque containing a charming little lake (Bench Lake) lies on the extreme end of the ridge just under Kootenai Peak. The walls of this cirque rise at the highest point 2,000 feet above the lake. One of the largest cirques in the drainage basin is that lying southwest of Campbell Mountain. It is fully 2 miles wide from north to south, and a second small cirque, with walls 600 or 700 feet high, has been developed in its floor. These cirques can be reached only by a hard climb and consequently they have rarely been seen.

Geologic features.—The Lewis overthrust fault, which is so prominent a feature along the east front of the mountains, crosses Little Kootenai Valley near the lower end of Waterton Lake, in Canadian territory. The limestone on the upper side of the fault shows on both sides of Waterton Lake in a great upfold or anticline. It is exposed at the mouth of the creek at the upper end of the lake, and it is also visible along the west shore for a distance of 2 miles south of the boundary line. North of that line it makes the mountain front on both sides of the valley.

The great syncline or downfold which has produced the Flattop Basin, as explained on a previous page, is well shown on the south side of Porcupine Ridge. Plate XII, *A*, is a view of this ridge from the

GREAT CIRQUE WALL ON NORTH SIDE OF GOATHAUNT MOUNTAIN.

Part shown is 1,200 feet high. Photograph by Bailey Willis.

highland between Valentine Creek and its South Fork. It shows a structure section nearly across the basin.

The band of intrusive diabase and the lava bed previously described show at many places on the ridge west of the main stream. The diabase is exposed on Olson Creek about 40 feet above the trail, at the first lake encountered in ascending the stream. From this place it rises toward the west above Brown Pass, showing a few hundred feet above the pass in the ridge to the north and at the foot of the glacier in the ridge to the south. The lava bed is considerably above the diabase and is present only in the high knobs of Porcupine Ridge and the ridge north of Brown Pass. It caps the small knob between the forks of Valentine Creek and shows in the low saddle in the ridge to the south. It also comes up on the northeast side of the basin or syncline and is well exposed on the point southeast of Bench Lake.

McDONALD VALLEY.

McDonald Creek is the largest stream in the park, and as it drains most of the central area between the Lewis and Livingston ranges it is the park's natural gateway or entrance. Not only is its valley favorably located, but it contains the largest lake in the park—Lake McDonald.

Trails and camps.—The traveler wishing to visit Lake McDonald and go up into the mountains beyond it leaves the railway at Belton, taking a stage which reaches the lake by a 3-mile drive over an excellent road. He then goes by boat to the upper end of the lake. From this point he must continue his journey on horseback, for beyond the lake there are no roads and few trails. He may take the trail from Glacier Hotel over Gunsight Pass to the St. Mary Valley, stopping on the way at the Sperry camp, or he may elect to follow the trail up McDonald Valley to the mouth of Mineral Creek and then climb the mountain to the right, across Swiftcurrent Pass, descending into Swiftcurrent Valley. Should he wish, however, to camp in Granite Park so as to enjoy more of the beauty of the mountain summits he can spend one day to good advantage in a trip to Ahern Pass, but by no means should he attempt that pass except on foot, as the trail beyond is merely a goat trail and is decidedly unsafe for a horse. Instead of going to Granite Park he may desire to explore farther north, and in that event he can proceed up Mineral Creek, cross Flattop Mountain, and descend to Waterton Lake, near the Canadian line. This route affords an opportunity to camp on Flattop, which, though not mountainous, is one of the most delightful spots in the park. For such a camp he can find water near the trail at a place known by all old-time guides as Kipp's cabin, or he can go to a small lake just east of Trapper Peak. From either of these camp sites he can ride for hours through a gently rolling, open woodland which rivals in beauty those parks that show the art of the landscape gardener at its best and in which pack and saddle horses may revel in luxuriant grass.

The traveler who does not wish to go much farther into the mountain region than the upper end of Lake McDonald may visit several interesting places, making the trip going and returning to the lake the same day. The most desirable ride, so far as scenery is concerned, is the trip to Avalanche Lake. This lake is one of the most picturesque in the park and well repays even a short visit. Good fishing may be found in the lakes in Camas Valley, to the west, or the small lake in Little St. Mary Valley, to the east.

The only wagon road in the park is the one from Belton to Apgar, at the foot of Lake McDonald, and thence nearly to the Canadian line by way of Flathead River.

There is no forage for stock at the head of Lake McDonald, so that hay must be shipped in. Above the lake there is no forage nearer than Granite Park or Flattop Mountain.

The traveler can be accommodated in comfortable chalets at Belton and in Glacier Hotel, at the head of Lake McDonald. Other accommodations may be had at the head of the lake and at Apgar.

The form of the valley.—This valley differs in form from others near by, as it has much open, rolling ground in its upper part. The lower part of the valley, up to the sharp bend near Haystack Butte, is much like the other valleys of this region. It is bounded by steep mountain walls, which are generally smooth and rounded, and the valley floor, though much narrower than many smaller valleys, is distinctly U shaped in cross section. Above the sharp bend just mentioned the immediate valleys of the streams are deep and rounded, but they are flanked by or rather cut in the relatively flat land forming Flattop Mountain and Granite Park.

Flattop Mountain is a mountain in name only, or by comparison with the valleys which are cut into it. When compared with the surrounding peaks it resembles the flat bottom of a basin. The basin extends from Haystack Butte and Heavens Peak on the south across the Continental Divide to Jefferson Pass on the north and from the Lewis Range on the east to the Livingston Range on the west. The floor of the basin has an altitude of about 6,500 feet. Although now considerably diversified it was doubtless at one time, long ago, a broad, gently undulating surface. Since then the streams have carved deep channels in that even floor, leaving Flattop Mountain, Granite Park, and other remnants of the old valley bottom here and there. On these rolling uplands the forest is open or lacking and the traveler can ride at will through a vast territory that resembles a carefully kept park in which the flowers are so abundant at certain seasons as to make the open vistas blaze with color.

Lakes.—Singularly there are few small lakes in this valley, but Lake McDonald makes up for any deficiency. It is an entrancing sheet of water, its only drawback being that it does not extend into the mountains. Its upper end is at their southwestern margin, and delightful views of their rugged heights may be obtained from almost any point on the lake or along its shore, but, unlike Lake St. Mary, it is not walled round or apparently overhung by high peaks.

Lake McDonald owes its origin to the great glacier that once flowed down the valley, but whether the water simply gathered in a basin scooped by the ice out of the solid rock or whether it is held in place by morainic material carried down by the ice has not been determined. It seems possible that the lake basin was formed in both ways.

Many rumors have been in circulation regarding the great depth of this lake, some putting it as much as 1,800 feet. Recently, however, it has been sounded and found to have a maximum depth of 440 feet. Its bottom is remarkably uniform throughout but is slightly lower near the head of the lake.

Avalanche Lake (Pl. VI, *B*) is a jewel set in rugged cirque walls and heavily timbered slopes. Another lake that drains into this valley is, on account of its peculiar position, one of the most remarkable in the park. This is Hidden Lake, which is well named, for, although it is practically on top of the Continental Divide, north of Sperry Glacier, it is almost completely concealed by high mountains.

Mountains.—Most of the mountain peaks in and around this valley, on account of their proximity to the settlements and roads, have been named, but none of them fall into the class of high peaks (over 10,000 feet). The highest summit on the rim of the valley is Mount Gould, altitude 9,544 feet, but Heavens and Longfellow peaks, on the west side, by virtue of their isolation seem to be much higher.

Glaciers.—Sperry Glacier, which is reached by a climb of nearly 1,500 feet from Sperry camp, on the head of Sprague Creek, is the largest in this drainage basin. It is about 1½ miles in width at its widest point and 1 mile long. It is an excellent example of a bench glacier, but is not so attractive as Blackfeet Glacier, on the other side of Gunsight Pass. There are only a few other glaciers in this basin, for the only place at which they could develop is on the east front of the Livingston Range, and most of this range is not high enough to support them.

Cirques.—Although the present glaciers in this basin are few in number, the old glaciers, as attested by the great cirques which they cut, were numerous and of large size. The most noted cirque is that which holds Avalanche Lake, and as it is connected with the main trail along McDonald Creek and is not far from Glacier Hotel it has been visited by many travelers. It is one of the deepest and at the same time one of the most symmetrical cirques to be found in the mountains. The back wall ranges in height from 2,000 to 3,500, and, although it is not so steep as some cirque walls in other valleys, little vegetation grows upon it, and to climb it is all but impossible. A noteworthy compound cirque lies just across the summit of Mount Brown, at the head of Snyder Creek. Both parts of it are symmetrical in plan and are surrounded by very steep walls. The wall back of the lower cirque is only about 500 feet high, but that surrounding the upper cirque ranges from 1,500 to 3,000 feet. Hidden Lake, like Avalanche Lake, lies in a cirque cut by an old glacier, but this cirque is long and narrow, as if the cutting had begun at the north end and progressed toward the south until it reached its present position. Another cirque worthy of mention lies just across the ridge north of Hidden Lake. It is cut deeply on the north side of the ridge, but, unlike the cirques just described, it has a strongly sloping floor, as if the glacier that originally carved it had cascaded down nearly to the bottom of the valley.

Geologic features.—The upper part of McDonald Valley, including Flattop Mountain, lies in the center of the great synclinal trough, the rocks on both sides dipping toward the medial line. The upturned beds on the east form the summit of the Lewis Range and those on the west form the summit of the Livingston Range. The bed of rock most noticed by the traveler is the sheet of lava that was long ago poured out in a molten condition on the bottom of the sea or lake in which the sediments that formed the mountain rocks were deposited. Since that time these rocks, together with the bed of lava, have been upturned or folded, and now all the beds dip in the same direction and at the same angle. The dark color and peculiar character of the lava rock generally attract the attention of the traveler, but the bad condition of the trail where it crosses the lava makes a much more vivid and lasting impression. The lava is well shown just west of Swiftcurrent Pass and also lower down, on the Granite Park trail. It is rough and dangerous where it is crossed by the trail to Ahern Pass and is prominent along the trail across Flattop Mountain. It also shows on West Flattop Mountain about a mile east of Trapper Peak, but here it is seldom seen, as it is far from the regular route of travel. Curiously Granite Park was so named on account of the prominent outcrop of the lava in its upper part. The early prospectors and trappers doubtless recognized this rock as crystalline and different from the limestone, argillite, and quartzite of the ordinary mountain rocks, and so they supposed it to be granite, but it is evident at a glance that such an identification is erroneous.

Prospecting.—Some of the first prospecting in the park was done in the valley of Mineral Creek, where a large amount of money has been expended in a search for copper ore. The zone of faults and dikes described as crossing the head of Swiftcurrent Creek is also found on Mineral Creek and across Flattop Mountain. One large dike, on which prospecting has been done in Granite Park, crosses the Continental Divide from Grinnell Glacier and after passing through Granite Park can be seen in the southern point of Flattop Mountain. Another dike, which looks much more promising to the miner, crosses the range from Iceberg Lake, cutting through Ahern Pass and extending thence northwestward across Flattop near its north end and terminating on the north point of West Flattop. Extensive prospecting has been done on this dike in Ahern Pass, on Cattle Queen Creek, and on Flattop Mountain.

LITTLE ST. MARY VALLEY.

Most of Little St. Mary Valley is outside of the mountains proper and is therefore of little interest. Its head, however, lies among some of the most impressive scenery in the park, and as that part is traversed by the main Gunsight trail it is seen by many travelers.

One of the most attractive lakes in the park, lying at the extreme head of the valley directly under Gunsight Pass, was locally known as Lake Louise, but recently it has been rechristened Lake Ellen Wilson, for the wife of the President of the United States. This lake is charming in itself, but when it is seen in its rugged setting its beauty is greatly enhanced. It lies about 2,800 feet higher than Lake McDonald but is easily reached by a good trail from Glacier Hotel. Lake Ellen Wilson owes much of its beauty to the imposing peaks which tower above it on either hand—Gunsight Mountain on the west (9,250 feet) and Mount Jackson on the east (10,023 feet).

This valley is noted for the compound cirque at its head. Lake Ellen Wilson lies in a basin excavated by the ice from the solid rock, and just below the lower end of the lake there is another cirque whose bottom is occupied by a small lake and whose back wall is 1,400 feet high and almost vertical. The presence of two such cirques in one valley is striking and at once raises the question, How is it possible for a glacier to cut two cirques at different levels, especially where the rock is fairly homogeneous throughout? The manner in which it was done is not well understood and space will not permit presentation here of the various explanations that have been offered. A similar though not so striking compound cirque is present at the head of the east branch of the valley, but it is all but inaccessible.

HARRISON VALLEY.

The lower part of Harrison Valley can be reached by a trail that runs from the mouth of the creek to Harrison Lake, but the part above the lake is not accessible. The valley is more nearly V-shaped than most of the other valleys of the park, and therefore it seems possible either that the glacier which once occupied its head did not extend far down the valley or else that the glacier was so small that it had little effect in modifying the original angular outline. The region has not been studied closely enough to determine this point, and as there are few trails it will probably be some time before it will be examined in detail.

Harrison Lake is one of the most attractive features of the valley and can be reached by the trail from the mouth of the creek, but it is best seen from the high ridges on either side or from some distant peak.

This valley heads between two of the most imposing peaks of the region, Mount Jackson (10,023 feet) on the west and Blackfeet Mountain (9,591 feet) on the east. It is deeply cut even to its head, the valley floor lying 5,400 feet or more than a mile below the summit of Mount Jackson, and 4,000 feet below the summit of Blackfeet Mountain.

The most interesting feature of the valley is Harrison Glacier (Pl. IX, A), at its upper end. This mass of ice is about 2 miles in linear extent and is perhaps the second in size in the park. It can be seen only from the Continental Divide above Blackfeet Glacier.

The greatest cirque in the valley is the one at its head, whose walls rise to the Continental Divide, 4,000 feet above. The walls slope considerably, but nevertheless they are very impressive when seen from the high points around the rim of the cirque. A few small cirques are perched on the sides of the valley, the one just south of Mount Thompson being the most interesting. Here the original cirque seems to have been on the Nyack Creek side, but at a later date another one was started on the west side of the ridge and this one cut through the intervening wall, so that the two merge. The later cirque is 500 feet lower than the older one. The rounded form of the ravine below the cirque indicates that the glacier cascaded down to the bottom of the valley.

NYACK VALLEY.

Nyack Creek is one of the largest streams in the park, and its valley was probably the first to be explored by a white man. In October, 1853, A. W. Tinkham, a civil engineer engaged with a Government party in explorations for the best route for the Pacific railroad, was ordered to examine Marias Pass. He came from the Bitterroot Valley, ascended Flathead River and its Middle Fork, and by mistake proceeded up Nyack Creek, thinking that he was on his way to the pass. He crossed the Cut Bank summit on October 20 but reported that it was impracticable as a railroad route.

A.   ONE OF THE LOBES OF HARRISON GLACIER.

From Continental Divide southeast of Mount Jackson.   Photograph by W. C. Alden.

B.   SMALL LAKE IN CAMAS VALLEY AT FOOT OF HEAVENS PEAK.

At the head of the lake there are a good camp ground and a meadow that affords plenty of pasture for stock.
Photograph by M. R. Campbell.

VIEW FROM CUT BANK PASS LOOKING WEST.

Mount Stimpson is the high peak in the center, Mount Pinchot the saddle mountain to the left, Eaglehead Mountain the pyramid in the distance. Mount Phillips on the extreme left, and Blackfeet Mountain and Pumpelly Glacier on the extreme right. Cut Bank Pass was crossed by Lieut. Tinkham in 1853. Photograph by M. R. Campbell.

Trails.—Mr. Tinkham, in ascending Nyack Creek, followed an Indian trail, so it is evident that this valley was a route of travel before the advent of the white man and probably had been used by the Indians for generations previous to that time. Mr. Tinkham reports no grass from the place where Belton now stands to the summit of the mountain, and in this respect there has been no change in the last 60 years. The lack of pasture is a serious drawback to travel in this valley, and on that account few people use the trail. Recently a new trail has been partly opened from Nyack Creek across the Continental Divide to Red Eagle Valley, but it is in poor condition and has been utilized by only a few of the more hardy travelers. A poor trail also continues up Nyack Creek beyond the Cut Bank trail and crosses into Two Medicine Valley by way of Dawson Pass, but in its present condition it is scarcely passable.

Mountains.—Nyack Valley is surrounded by a rim of high mountains, but there is only one peak that may be regarded as of first rank. This is Mount Stimpson, which stands 10,155 feet above the level of the sea. Other peaks of importance are Mounts Pinchot (9,332 feet), Phillips (9,485 feet), and Blackfeet (9,591 feet). (See Pl. X.)

Glaciers.—Pumpelly Glacier is the largest in the valley and is so named from the fact that it was seen and described by Prof. Raphael Pumpelly in a trip across this pass in 1883. It is nearly 2 miles in length and in reality forms part of a single great mass of ice called by the names Blackfeet, Harrison, and Pumpelly glaciers. A moderate-sized glacier lies on the north side of Mount Thompson, and four small glaciers hug the northeast side of Mount Stimpson.

Cirques.—Cirques abound in this valley, but none of them are so well known as the cirques of other valleys in the park. The one which lies on the west side of Mount Stimpson is probably the most striking, having a back wall 4,000 feet high. Between Mount Phillips and Mount Pinchot two cirques probably have been cut from opposite sides until they have united, forming a low saddle called Surprise Pass. This pass is not well known, for it is difficult to reach, there being no trail leading across from Nyack Creek to Coal Creek.

COAL VALLEY.

General description.—The valley of Coal Creek, although embracing considerable territory, is not particularly attractive because of its lack of striking features such as lakes, glaciers, and glacial cirques. Moreover, it has no trails and it is doubtful if trails will be constructed in it in the near future.

The creek was so named because a coal bed, which occurs in soft lake beds of Tertiary age, outcrops near its mouth. The beds associated with the coal are probably the same as the soft rocks in the valley of Flathead River, which contain coal beds that are exposed at a number of places.

The valley of the North Fork of Coal Creek is sharply incised, showing that no glacier, or possibly a very small one, has passed down it, but the main valley is broad and rounded and its sides are scoured smooth, indicating that the valley must have been the outlet for a large amount of glacial ice.

Most of the high peaks in the southern part of the park, including those that can be seen from the railroad, are clustered round this basin. The most conspicuous is Mount Stimpson, which has an altitude of 10,155 feet. The other noteworthy peaks are Pinchot, Phillips, Eaglehead, and St. Nicholas. Mount St. Nicholas is one of the most striking pyramidal peaks in the region and when covered with snow seems like a giant spire reaching toward the heavens. This is the mountain generally seen from the railroad, and it never fails to attract the attention of the passing traveler.

There are only a few cirques in the valley, the most striking being the great one called Marthas Basin. It appears to be an old cirque in which smaller ones have been cut. The one in the southwest corner is marked by a small lake, behind which the walls rise steeply to the summit of Eaglehead Mountain, 3,000 feet above.

PARK VALLEY.

The valley of Park Creek is easily reached from the town of Essex, on the railroad, or from Two Medicine Valley by a climb over Two Medicine Pass. It has few features of interest except some small cirques or "parks" and a few prominent peaks on the rim, but none of these can be reached from the trail.

The peaks having altitudes of more than 9,000 feet are Mount St. Nicholas, 9,385 feet; Mount Rockwell, 9,255 feet; and Mount Grizzly, 9,075 feet. Of these St. Nicholas is by far the most conspicuous, and probably some day a trail will be made to Rotunda Cirque, which will enable the traveler to camp within reach of the peak and to see the beautiful view from its summit.

There are several interesting cirques in this valley, which are difficult of access but which when once attained will be found to be open glades filled with flowers. Some of them contain small lakes. Rotunda Cirque, the most conspicuous, is compound and in one of the lobes there is an attractive lake.

OLE VALLEY.

Ole Valley is even less interesting than that of Park Creek or Coal Creek and it is not accessible by trail from any quarter. Although uninviting in its lack of scenic charm, it contains a geologic feature of the greatest interest. The Lewis overthrust fault, as shown on the map, extends along the east front of the mountains from the Canadian line as far as Squaw Mountain, back of Glacier Park station. From this point it swings to the southwest along the mountain ridge which lies just north of and parallel with the railroad track, passing the summit and finally crossing the railroad and valley at Fielding, 20 miles west of Glacier Park station. The fault plane dips about 10° NW. and passes from a point near the top of Summit Mountain into the valley of Ole Creek at a height so great that it is exposed in the head of the valley for a distance of 3 or 4 miles. In other words, the creek has cut a hole in the overthrust mountain rocks and into the soft rocks of the plains. Although normally the mountain rocks belong many thousands of feet below the plains rocks, they have been thrust over the rocks of the plains and the stream has simply exposed the abnormal relation.

CAMAS VALLEY.

Camas Valley is easily reached, for the main road up the valley of Flathead River crosses Camas Creek about 10 miles northwest of Belton. From this road a well-used trail extends up the valley and across the ridge on the east to the head of Lake McDonald and a less used but still plain trail leads nearly to the head of the valley, where there is a low pass into the headwater region of McDonald Creek. This is reported to have been the route by which the Indians crossed the mountains from Flathead Lake, 30 miles southwest of the park, to Waterton Lake, and it was followed by Lieut. Ahern and Prof. Culver in August, 1890. The valley contains a number of ranches between the main road and Rogers ranch, but above that place it is heavily timbered and affords little pasturage except at the head of the third lake, where there is a fine meadow. Some grass can probably also be found above the next lake, but that is rather difficult to reach and the amount of pasture is uncertain.

There are six small lakes in the valley, three of which are located in the lower part and are easily reached by trail from Lake McDonald. (See Pl. IX, B.) The lakes in the upper part of the valley are not on any regular trail, but the forest on the south slope is open and probably would present little difficulty to the traveler who desires to pay them a visit. The upper lakes occupy deep cirques at the foot of Longfellow Peak, but the others probably rest in rock basins scooped out by the glacier that once nearly filled the valley and flowed out into the broad, open valley of Flathead River. Many travelers stopping on Lake McDonald visit these lakes to enjoy the fine fishing for which they are noted.

That part of Camas Valley which lies in the mountains is deep and narrow, and the peaks, although not the largest in the region, seem to tower above it to a great height. Heavens and Longfellow peaks are the most prominent. The summit of the former is almost 6,000 feet above the little lake at its base, and the latter stands 4,000 feet above the lake occupying the lower cirque. The bent and contorted strata in McPartland' Mountain look particularly rugged and imposing from the third lake, but with the exception of this belt of distorted rocks, which passes through McPartland Mountain and Longfellow Peak, the rocks dip moderately and regularly toward the northeast.

The compound cirque at the east foot of Longfellow Peak is the most striking in the valley, and its western wall, about 4,000 feet high, is extremely rugged and almost vertical. A pretty little cirque holding the Dutch Lakes lies at the head of Dutch Creek, on the south side of this peak.

LOGGING VALLEY.

The valley of Logging Creek extends only a short distance into the mountains, but its upper end is very rugged and picturesque as seen from the bordering summits or from the lake itself. It was named about 30 years ago, when it was the scene of extensive logging operations, which, however, proved to be a failure, as is attested by the many rotting logs still to be seen in this vicinity.

Recently a good trail has been cut from Adair across the point of Adair Ridge to the foot of the lake, where good grazing can be found. The valley is otherwise inaccessible except by boat.

Logging Lake, over 6 miles in length, has rarely been visited except by fishermen. It lies almost entirely outside of the mountains and in other less fortunate regions would be regarded as beautiful, but here there are so many more picturesque lakes that this one has been neglected. Grace Lake, which is smaller, lies a mile or more above Logging Lake but can be seen only from the surrounding heights, as it is practically encircled by heavy, impenetrable forest.

Although the head of the valley is cut deep in the Livingston Range, there are no commanding peaks about it. Vulture Peak, on the north side, is the highest, standing 9,611 feet above sea level, or 5,800 feet above Logging Lake.

Vulture Glacier, on the south side of the peak, is the largest in the valley, being about a mile wide and about the same in length. A small glacier lying just east of the large one, but not represented on the map, has the distinction of being the only glacier in the park that discharges its waters above ground into both the Atlantic and the Pacific oceans. It is therefore called Two Ocean Glacier. (See Pl. XI, A.)

The most striking cirque in Logging Valley is the one at the head of the valley, in which doubtless originated a large glacier that once moved out from this mountain center, rounding and smoothing the

A. CONTINENTAL DIVIDE AT HEAD OF LOGGING CREEK.

Vulture Peak just visible on the left; below it the south end of Two Ocean Glacier, which discharges to the right into the Hudson Bay drainage basin and to the left into streams that lead to the Pacific Ocean. Photograph by M. R. Campbell.

B. FORDING THE OUTLET OF BOWMAN LAKE.

Kintla Peak, white with snow, on the extreme left. Photograph by M. R. Campbell.

valley sides and scooping out the basin now occupied by Logging Lake. About 1,300 feet above the bottom of this cirque there is a great flat shelf of solid rock, which is bounded by sharp walls and was cut by some small glacier, probably at a later date. This glacier worked back so far to the north that it cut through the narrow divide between it and a cirque opening to the east and formed the broad flat which now marks the summit of the pass. Perhaps the best example of the circular cuts made by glaciers into a high mountain is afforded by the peak about 2 miles southwest of Vulture Glacier. These cirques have been cut from four directions into the peak, which has thus been reduced to only a fraction of its former magnitude. The cuts are not flat-bottomed like typical cirques, but they have the circular shape indicating a glacial origin.

QUARTZ VALLEY.

Quartz Creek derives its name from a prominent ledge of white quartz that occurs in a small lake at the extreme headwaters of the creek just east of Vulture Peak. The valley is wide and open as far up as the upper end of the lower lake, and there is a ranch about 3 miles above the main valley road.

Trails.—A good trail extends from the mouth of the creek to the lower end of the main lake and a poor one crosses the ridge from Lower Quartz Lake to the foot of Bowman Lake. Grass is abundant in the valley below the lakes, but in the upper part the timber is very thick and heavy and there is no pasture except possibly at the extreme head of the valley. Formerly there was a trail along the south shore of Quartz Lake to the head of the valley, but as it was cut almost the entire distance in heavy timber it is difficult to keep open. At last accounts it was so much obstructed by fallen trees that a horse could not be taken above the lower end of the lake. Sooner or later, however, a good trail will be built up the north side of the valley to Cerulean Lake and thence across the summit just north of Bighorn Peak. Such a trail would open many beautiful views and afford many excellent sites on which to pitch camp.

Lakes.—There are four very attractive lakes in this valley. The three that are generally seen have not received distinctive names and are known as Quartz, Middle Quartz, and Lower Quartz lakes. The lower lake is shallow and is not particularly attractive, as it lies entirely outside of the high mountains; the middle lake is small but probably very deep; and the upper lake is a beautiful sheet of water 4 miles long and 254 feet deep in the deepest place. Two miles above this lies Cerulean Lake, a small body of water sheltered by some of the most imposing mountain walls to be found in the park. This lake has doubtless been visited by very few people, as it is practically inaccessible, but it can be readily seen from the Continental Divide, on the east.

Mountains.—The valley of Quartz Creek is flanked by three high peaks—Vulture on the south and Rainbow and Carter on the north. Vulture Peak is not so high as the other two, but it is more imposing from this valley, as it rises in a solid wall a mile above the level of the lake. The other points that appear so prominent from below are seen by one standing on a commanding eminence on the surrounding wall to be only low spurs of the higher peaks.

Glaciers.—Two or three small glaciers lying on the east side of Vulture Peak drain into Quartz Valley, but these are insignificant compared with Rainbow Glacier, which occupies a similar position on Rainbow Peak. This glacier is about a mile square and is an imposing sight from the Continental Divide, to the east. The glacier lies on an enormous shelf draining into Cerulean Lake, at least 2,000 feet below. The ice comes to the very edge of the precipice, but seldom, if ever, does a block fall into the deep-blue waters of the lake.

Cirques.—A great cirque, beside which all others in this valley seem dwarfed, contains Cerulean Lake. Its walls are from 2,000 to 4,300 feet in height and inclose the cirque on three sides.

Moraines.—Few well-marked terminal moraines cross any of the main valleys in the park. The ice in the glacial epoch was at least 2,500 feet deep in many of the large valleys, and it must have carried down with it immense quantities of rock fragments and fine material. In many places this débris was swept away by the flood of water that issued from the front of the glacier, but in a few valleys the material was preserved and to-day is visible as great ridges stretching across the valleys and up the slopes on either side. One of the most perfect moraines of the park was dumped across Quartz Valley above Lower Quartz Lake. It is in two parts—one below the middle lake and the other above that and at the foot of the upper lake. As the water in the upper lake is 254 feet deep, it seems probable that the portion of the moraine below water level is at least that height, and it is 200 feet more above that level. The surface of the moraine is pitted and hummocky, having a typical morainic topography.

Mining.—Although little prospecting has been done in this part of the park, it is probable that the first mineral discovery in the region was made at the head of Quartz Creek, where the great quartz vein is exposed. This vein carries a small quantity of copper ore, and as it is exceedingly prominent it was probably discovered at an early date. From this locality prospecting was extended to the east and carried on in a more systematic manner, but with little better success, and finally almost all the claims were abandoned.

BOWMAN VALLEY.

At present Bowman Valley is, next to the valley of McDonald Creek, the principal line of travel on the west side of the range. The valley is broad and open and it was evidently deeply scoured by the great glacier that formerly extended out from the center of the range into the broad valley of Flathead River.

Trails.—From the main road in Flathead Valley a wagon road leads up Bowman Creek to the foot of the lake, from which an excellent trail extends up the west side of the lake to a point within about 2½ miles of its head. Above this point the trail is passable, but in places is very rough and narrow. It extends up the main creek to Hole-in-the-Wall Falls, where it turns to the right and climbs over the Continental Divide through Brown Pass. About a mile and a quarter above Bowman Lake a well-worn trail turns to the right, ascending the fork of the creek that heads in Jefferson Pass, but within a distance of about 2 miles the trail is lost in heavy timber. It is reported that pack horses have been taken over the pass, but the traveler should not undertake the trip unless he is prepared to spend the night in the woods and cut a trail most of the way. A poor trail leads from the foot of the lake (Pl. XI, *B*) across the ridge on the east to Lower Quartz Lake, but the trail is very steep and on the far side of the ridge can scarcely be followed. The best camp site in the valley is at the foot of the lake, where grass, wood, and water are abundant and the fishing is good. Above this point there is no grass except a little in the bottom of the valley near Hole-in-the-Wall Falls, but a good camp can be made in Brown Pass. If it is late in the season and the creek is dry, by turning to the south and climbing the hill a fair camping spot may be found just under the glacier.

Lakes.—Bowman Lake, the only lake in this valley, is 7 miles long and from half to three-quarters of a mile wide. Soundings show that the bottom of the lake is remarkably smooth and regular and that the greatest depth is 256 feet. Throughout the upper half of the lake the trail follows closely the west shore, affording many beautiful views of the snow-capped summit of Rainbow Peak reflected in the lake, or, in case a storm suddenly sweeps down from the mountains, a chance to get wet feet by the dashing of the waves.

Mountains.—The high mountains surrounding this valley are Rainbow Peak and Mount Carter on the east and an unnamed high ridge on the west. Rainbow Peak, standing 5,840 feet above the lake, is without doubt the dominating feature of Bowman Valley. As seen from the lower end of the lake it is particularly imposing, but if covered by a fresh fall of snow it glistens in the sunlight and seems to pierce the sky. The peak was named from the fancied resemblance of the banded rocks near the summit to a rainbow. In near-by views the resemblance is not striking, but at a distance it is said to be fairly strong.

Late in the afternoon, when the sun is low in the west, its slanting rays bring out each rugged detail of spire and pinnacle, buttress and battlement, on a mountain at the head of the valley that, on account of its form and sculpture, should be known as Castle Mountain. This peak can be climbed from a camp in Brown Pass and will well repay the effort.. The traveler should keep around the mountain to the right, crossing the foot of a large snow bank lying beneath the little glacier at the end of the peak. After surmounting the long spur that projects toward the northwest he will find a goat trail which can be followed around the mountain for a distance of at least 3 miles. From this path the traveler can obtain an excellent view of the lakes, glaciers, and peaks on all sides and can look down into the valley of Bowman Creek, nearly a mile below him.

Glaciers.—No large glaciers drain into Bowman Creek, but there are a number of small ones on the west wall of the valley and one or two on the east. Baby and Boulder glaciers are the most prominent on the west, the latter being remarkable in that it extends across the summit and discharges both ways. (See Pl. XII, *B*.) The principal glacier on the east side lies directly under Mount Carter and is one of the most notable cascading glaciers in the park. It lies in a small cirque and finds an outlet through a narrow channe' falling at least 500 feet.

Cirques.—The most prominent cirque in the valley is that at its extreme head. This cirque is compound, the two parts being separated by a vertical wall 2,000 feet in height. A small stream which drains the upper cirque finds an outlet through an opening in the limestone and plunges into the lower cirque from a crevice in the rock. From this fact it is known as Hole-in-the-Wall Falls.

Moraines.—Bowman Lake probably owes its existence to the presence of a rock basin scooped out by the ice and also to the great moraine which the glacier built across the valley at its lower end. The moraine consists of two parallel ridges, at least 100 feet high, which descend from the valley wall on the west side and continue as far as the creek. The surfaces of the ridges are marked by pits and hummocks characteristic of the topography of a morainic belt.

KINTLA VALLEY.

Kintla Valley lies near the Canadian line and is separated from Bowman Valley by a great mass of rugged mountains. It is far from the frequented routes of travel and on this account is rarely seen by travelers.

Trails.—The lower end of Kintla Lake is about $1\frac{1}{2}$ miles from the main wagon road up the valley of Flathead River. A trail from this

A. PORCUPINE RIDGE, FROM HIGHLAND BETWEEN VALENTINE CREEK AND ITS SOUTH FORK.

The Guardhouse in the center and Jefferson Pass on the left. The heavy limestone showing in the dip slope on the left can be followed by the eye throughout most of the length of Porcupine Ridge. The open parklike country in the foreground affords excellent sites for camps and grass for stock. Photograph by E. M. Parks.

B. BOULDER GLACIER AND CIRQUE WALL AT HEAD OF BOWMAN VALLEY.

From east wall of cirque, above Hole-in-the-Wall Falls. Boulder Glacier with Kintla Peak towering back of it on the extreme left, Boundary Mountains in the center, and great cirque wall above Nos Lake on the right. Photograph by W. C. Alden.

road leads up the north side of the lake and follows the creek up to Upper Kintla Lake and passes along its north shore. Above this lake the trail is uncertain. It is reported as climbing to the Continental Divide just north of the international boundary. A branch trail is also said to ascend from the upper lake to Agassiz Glacier. Good camp sites can be found at the old oil well at the upper end of Kintla Lake. It seems probable that in the near future a trail will be cut from this valley across the summit to Boundary Creek, all within the park. When this is done the valley can be easily reached and doubtless will be visited by many travelers and receive the recognition that its rugged and beautiful features deserve.

Lakes.—There are two lakes in Kintla Valley which compare favorably with any other lakes in the park. The lower lake lies entirely outside of the mountains, but the upper lake is surrounded by some of the highest peaks. When the valley becomes more accessible to the traveler these lakes are destined to become very popular resorts.

Mountains.—The highest mountain peak on the border of this valley is Kintla Peak, which stands at an altitude of 10,100 feet above the sea, or 5,730 feet above the surface of Upper Kintla Lake. Although this peak is the highest in the vicinity, it is by no means so striking as the sharp pyramidal peak about a mile to the north. This is one of the most symmetrical peaks in the park and is a conspicuous object from almost any point of view.

Glaciers.—The great group of mountains lying between Bowman and Kintla valleys contains a correspondingly large group of glaciers, which are second in size only to the Blackfeet and associated glaciers farther south. The best known of these is Agassiz Glacier, which can be reached on foot from a camp at Brown Pass. It is true that such a trip would require some rather rough mountain climbing, but it presents no serious difficulties to those accustomed to such recreation. Agassiz Glacier is about $1\frac{1}{2}$ miles wide and terminates in a pronounced valley glacier or ice tongue at least half a mile in length. Kintla Glacier, just across the ridge to the west, is not so easily reached, and consequently has not been visited by many travelers. This body of ice is at least 2 miles wide and 1 mile long. In addition to these principal glaciers there are a few small ones in other parts of the basin.

Cirques.—The two large glaciers just mentioned lie in cirques cut near the crest of the main ridge, upon which they rest. Below them are older cirquelike valleys that are very much deeper and more extensive than the cirques of the present glaciers. Each tributary of the stream heads in a similar cirque, showing that at the time when these were formed the great glacier that flowed out of the valley was composed of several branches, each of which headed in a cirque at about the same level.

Oil wells.—No mining has been carried on in this valley. A well was drilled for oil at the upper end of Kintla Lake, where there is a seep of oil which has been known since the first settlement of the country. Another well was drilled on Flathead River about a mile below the mouth of Kintla Creek, where there was no surface indication of oil. According to the most reliable reports no oil was found in either of these wells.

O